THE GIRLS' GUIDE TO ROCKING

HOW TO START A BAND, BOOK GIGS, AND GET ROLLING TO ROCK STARDOM

★★★

JESSICA HOPPER

WORKMAN PUBLISHING ★ NEW YORK

Library of Congress Cataloging-in-Publication Data

Hopper, Jessica.
The girls' guide to rocking : how to start a band, book gigs, and
get rolling to rock stardom / by Jessica Hopper.
p. cm.
ISBN 978-0-7611-5141-8 (alk. paper)   1.   Rock groups--Vocational
guidance--Juvenile literature.   2.   Women rock musicians--Vocational
guidance--Juvenile literature.   I.   Title.
ML3795.H775 2008
782.42166023--dc22   2008052803

Cover design: Robb Allen / Book design: Rae Ann Spitzenberger

Workman books are available at special discounts when purchased in bulk for
premiums and sales promotions as well as for fund-raising or educational use.
Special editions or book excerpts can also be created to specification.
For details, contact the Special Sales Director at the address below.

WORKMAN PUBLISHING COMPANY, INC.
225 Varick Street
New York, NY 10014-4381
www.workman.com

Printed in the United States of America
First printing April 2009
10 9 8 7 6 5 4 3 2 1

"I wasn't born to be a spectator."

PATTI SMITH, 1975

ACKNOWLEDGMENTS

My deepest thanks to my editor Megan Nicolay, whose vision and faith made this book possible, and to everyone at Workman, especially Rae Ann Spitzenberger, Danielle Hark, Anne Kerman, Beth Levy, Jarrod Dyer, and Andrea Bussell for their toil and enthusiasm. Thanks to Franz Nicolay for hooking it up.

This book would not be what it is if not for the writers who provided research assistance: Nikki Darling, Beth Capper, J.R. Nelson, and John MacDonald.

Anaheed Alani, Liz Armstrong, Miles Raymer, Aaron Rose, Mike Taylor, Al Burian, David Scheid, Paul Sommerstein, Adam Shore, Josh Davison, Katie Rose, and Seb Roberts all provided invaluable input to the manuscript. I am especially grateful to Becky Smith, Morgan Thoryk, and Joan Hiller for their tremendous dedication to this book.

Thank you to Greg Gillis, Jenn Nuccio, Carianne and Kenny Laguna, Joan Jett, Karla Schickele and the Willie Mae Rock Camp, and Girls Rock Philly for your kind words, and Nedelle Torrisi for use of yours. Thanks to Dan Monick and Mike Dewitt for your photos.

I am indebted to the following folks for sharing their expertise and answering questions: David Scott Stone, Noah Leger, Britt Daniel, Craig Finn, Nora Brank, Ellie Erickson, Adam Pfahler, Tim Iseler, Jeff Parker, Jonah Bayer, Teeter Sperber, Lisa Bralts-Kelly, Kiki Yablon, Curt Cameruci, Ben Dickey, Jonah Matranga, Nick DeWitt, Arlie Carstens, Shayla Hason, Ben Fasman, Rjyan Kidwell, Bryan Christner, Jenny

Hoyston, Dan Korestsky, David Lewis, Fred Lonberg-Holm, Sam McPheeters, Peter Margasak, Trevor Kelly, Joe Plummer, Dean Spunt, Randy Randall, Eric Ziegenhagen, Daniel Littleton, Liz Mitchell, Andrea Zollo, Annie Clark, Nate Lepine, Dan Monick, Laurent Lebec, Mia Clarke. Special thanks to those who gave hours and days, freely and without complaint: Matthew Hale Clark, Jeremy Lemos, David Singer, Tim Kinsella, and Zach Goheen.

Stacey Graham, David Head, James Kennedy, Vell Mullens, Nadia Mizner, Tom Lynch, Louis Louis, Karissa Sutton, Amy Abts, Karl Schmidt, Russell Troyer, Kevin Erickson, Ryan P., William Melton, Jenn, Evan Mack, JR Robinson, Simon Cott, Chris Juarez, Liz Bustamante, Neil Harmsen, and The Go! Team,

generously supplied me with tips and info on equipment.

Thanks to my editors and employers— Kevin Williams at the *Chicago Tribune*, Randall Roberts at *LA Weekly*, Eric Grandy at *The Stranger*, Kiki Yablon, Alison True and Philip Montoro at the *Chicago Reader*, Jane Feltes and all the producers and staff of *This American Life*, and everyone at Plan B—for their patience and support.

To Annielaurie Erickson, Eve Sturges, Lena Singer, Jennifer Patton and family, Liz Hulsizer, Robin, Ian and Max Harris, Kells, Shae Jordan, The EPPC, Matt, Morgan, my Hopper and Redding families, for their hospitality and cheerleading, I am grateful.

This book is dedicated to the memories of Ellen Willis, Kristen Pfaff, Zola Eaton, and Helen Hopper.

TABLE OF CONTENTS

Patti LaBelle, Nona Hendryx, and Sarah Dash of pioneering glam funk group, Labelle, weren't afraid to express themselves.

Meg White of The White Stripes rocks out on the drums.

Taylor Swift began writing her own songs when she was twelve.

INTRODUCTION

I wound up playing guitar by accident. I was sitting in tenth-grade Health class, between my friends Ted and Andrew. They were my main sources for information about music, the closest thing I knew to experts because they had a band. "I want to play bass," I announced one day. "You can't play bass, your hands are too small. You won't be able to hold down the strings right," said Andrew. He made me hold my hands up to his as if to measure. He was a bass player, and even though he was terrible, this was his way of saying, "You must be *this* tall to ride the roller coaster." Never mind that if I'd had hands that big at fifteen I would have looked like a total freak. "You should get a guitar instead," Ted suggested. And so I did.

When I was young and first playing and forming basement bands with my best friends, I believed a lot of things that weren't true; in part because the only sources I had for information were boys like Andrew and Ted. Their idea about rock music and playing it was that there was only the right way and the wrong way. There were also a lot of arcane rules and things you had to blindly agree to. Like that Led Zeppelin's "Stairway to Heaven" was the best song ever written, that your hands must be a certain size to play the bass, and that you have to be a really good musician before you can start a band. It took a few years before I discovered that all these things were way wrong; and "Stairway to Heaven" isn't even the best Led Zeppelin song.

Here I am, fifteen years after that fateful Health class, and me and my little fingers have been playing guitar (*and* bass *and* drums *and* keyboards) in bands ever since. I've made records, toured in bands, played shows in every place imaginable, made T-shirts, flyers, and very good friends in the process. When I fell in love with music (ninth grade), I soon fell in love with the idea of making it, too. I didn't want to listen to songs; I wanted to participate. When I went to shows, I wanted to be onstage, too. Music became an obsession, and has been my whole life since then— and it's been rad.

I made this book for you so that you don't have to take the word of the two dudes on the JV Bowling team who sit next to you in Health class, so that you can turn your love of music—and desire to play it—into something real.

This book can guide you through the entire process—from dreaming up the kind of band you want to be in all the way to being in an established band, touring the world, and making business deals. For you, making music might be just a personal hobby, something you keep in your bedroom. Or maybe your dreams are of the arena-rock star variety. This book is a resource for you and your band, so that you're armed with all the knowledge you need to make those things happen for yourself—and that nothing will stand in your way.

When I first started playing, I felt like all the boys I knew were in on a world of top-secret information. I felt like I didn't have permission to enter that world. I didn't know if I would ever catch up or not feel a little lost. I loved music so much, all I wanted was to be part of it, I wanted to be making it, I was totally consumed by it. Over time, I realized that my love for music was all I really needed. That was my permission slip. I was already in the gang. This book is all the secrets, and also, your permission slip. Welcome to the gang.

CHAPTER 1

LET'S GET READY TO ROCK

Most rock bands have four basic parts—guitar, drums, bass, and vocals. This is the usual setup, because it covers all the bases: Guitar does the melody (the main tune), the drums provide rhythm, and the bass, doing both melody and rhythm, is the bridge between the two. Generally, for a band to be considered a "rock" band, you need to have an instrument playing melody and another doing the rhythm. Lots of bands have two guitars—one rhythm and the other lead. Keyboards (or piano) are also pretty common to the rock band lineup, sometimes replacing the guitar or bass. There are countless combinations of instruments, and as long as the music you're playing isn't easy-listening, you probably qualify as a rock band.

TAKE IT FROM THE TOP

Each instrument's sound depends on a zillion little factors: how well it was made, how old it is, how it's been taken care of, what kind of wood it's made from, what brand it is, what sort of amplifier and distortion pedals you play it through, what sort of sticks/picks/pickups/strings you use. Chances are, the first instrument you start playing on (unless someone hooked you up with something nice) will sound perfectly okay, but not amazing. Beginner models or cheap, used equipment is where everyone starts. My first guitar was $90 used, and I got a Fender practice amp from a garage sale for $15. That was my setup for the first few years, and it suited me just fine (after you've been playing for a year or two, you can get snobby about equipment).

PLAY WHAT YOUR MAMA GAVE YA

Just because most rock bands have a guitar-bass-drums setup doesn't mean you can't rock with other instruments. There is hardly any instrument that won't fit in a rock band (except maybe a tuba; they are pretty hard to make "rock"). If you already play something that isn't a traditional rock instrument, there is no reason that you can't play it in a rock band. There are plenty of bands that have violas, violins, or cellos. Steely Dan had a flugelhorn player, Bright Eyes has string players. Ian Anderson, the singer of chart-topping '70s rock band Jethro Tull, played the flute. He wore terrible-amazing fringed outfits, hopped around stage like an excited troll, and played one of the most non-rock instruments there is—and he was a superstar. There is absolutely no reason that you, with your flute-rocking skills, cannot be the Ian Anderson of tomorrow.

STRINGS, HORNS, AND OTHER ACOUSTIC INSTRUMENTS

For string players, if you are in a band with amplified instruments and/or a drummer, you will need to be amplified, too. Even if you play your cello as loud as you can, it's no match for a bass blaring out of an amp. With string instruments, you need a pre-amp and a pickup. A pickup senses the instrument or strings' vibrations, and the pre-amp makes them louder, so when you plug into an amplifier, you'll have a thick version of your instrument's natural sounds.

My friends who play cello and viola in rock bands all use piezoelectric ("piezo") pickups, which can be found online for about $20. These have a much fuller sound than the other pickups available for string instruments. An ART Tube MP

> "When I started ... writing songs like 'Just a Girl,' I suddenly saw mirror images of myself in the crowd. That was a very cool feeling."
>
> **GWEN STEFANI, NO DOUBT**

is a powerful pre-amp, and you can find one for around $30. You can also buy electric violins and cellos, but unless you are in a jazz-fusion band, they're weird and fake-sounding—and they look a little like crossbows.

With strings and other acoustic instruments, you want to stick with using pickups whenever you can, rather than putting a mic in front of it. If you are playing a live show and your acoustic guitar is mic'ed, you run the risk of having a lot of harsh, near constant feedback. With acoustic instruments in a rock setting, ask the sound person to turn you way up in the monitors so that you can hear yourself—though when you do this, you also run the risk of having a lot of feedback (that screechy, loud, high-pitched sound) because the microphone will pick up the sound blasting from the monitors. You will have to position or angle your instrument and microphone

away from the monitors so that you are feedback-free.

Many sound people in clubs won't automatically know how to work with your sound, so if you need to be loud, you have to speak up for yourself. You are going to be competing against blaring, electrified instruments and powerful amps. Do a sound check at show volume—get things nice and loud. You can always back off the mic if you need to be quieter.

FIY (FIND IT YOURSELF)

I got my first guitar when I was fifteen. I found it by calling around to stores and asking for the cheapest guitar they carried. I was in ninth grade and delivered papers for a living, so I wasn't exactly rolling in cash. A Guitar Center in a distant suburb had one for $90. I didn't ask what kind it was, since all that mattered was that I could afford it. I didn't know anything about guitars anyhow. My dad drove me out there, where I stared

YOUR GUITAR

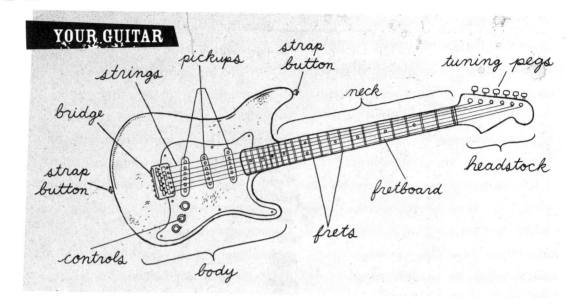

strings · pickups · strap button · tuning pegs · neck · bridge · strap button · controls · body · frets · fretboard · frets · headstock

at it intensely for two minutes before I purchased it without playing it. I wanted to seem like I knew what I was doing, and was deathly afraid (and too proud) to ask the sales dude questions. I was so nervous about somehow getting it all wrong that I *did* get it wrong: I walked out with my guitar in my arms like a baby and forgot to buy the cord, picks, strings, strap, *and* case.

Maybe you're an ice-cold lady of fierce confidence and aren't shedding a drop of sweat over your trip to the instrument plaza/Guitar Center—but if you are sweating it, when you go to buy your first drum kit or guitar, don't freak. Every musician since the beginning of time was, at one point, a beginner. Don't be ashamed that you don't know what you are doing yet, even if you walk into the store and the entire drum department is filled with guys playing insane solos while you aren't even sure what size sticks you need. Once you read this chapter, you will be fully prepared for your first fateful voyage to the guitar shop/drum zone/music emporium.

Beginner guitars, or "child model" guitars, are inexpensive because they are made from cheap, lightweight wood, which is why those guitars tend to have a thin, almost squeaky sound. My favorite guitar is a Teisco child's model guitar from 1971 that I got in eleventh grade. When played on its own through an amp, it sounds like a duck with a cold. When I play it through a distortion pedal or two, it sounds like a very bossy duck—and for this, I love the guitar even more. It's not the best, but it tries hard, and it's mine. When I first picked up drums, I went with the cheapest stuff I could get my hands on. You can upgrade from duck-squeak and super-used drumheads later. Learning to play on fancy, new, expensive equipment won't make you play any better or learn any faster.

GUITARS

The two things you're going to be checking for are whether the guitar is playable and that it works. Those sound like they're the same thing, but playability is really just about making sure the guitar is in good physical shape and that it's a match for you. Here's how:

1 Press the strings to the fret board. You should be able to press them down fairly easily, and there shouldn't be much space between the strings and the neck.

That space between the guitar and the strings is called the *action*. You want a guitar with medium to low action.

2 Examine the neck. It should be straight, with no bowing or warping. It's hard to tell just by looking; if the strings are buzzing and hitting the neck when you pluck them individually, it's probably warped.

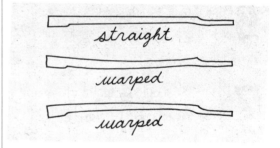

straight

warped

warped

3 Stand up with the guitar hanging on you. You should be able to easily reach the end of the neck. Depending on how long your arms are, you may need to be playing a three-quarter scale model. (A three-quarter model is just a little smaller than a regular size guitar; it doesn't look like you're playing a toy or anything.) You should feel comfortable wearing the guitar and strumming it. It should feel weighty but not heavy.

4 Check to make sure the frets are not worn all the way down. Run your hand up and down the neck. Each fret should be slightly raised, and you should feel a little bump when your hand goes over it.

5 Check that the guitar has all its tuning pegs and strings. A bass has four; guitars have six.

6 Look it over and make sure there are no cracks, missing chunks, or giant holes.

7 The guitar should be tuned. If it's not, have a salesperson tune it.

8 Test to make sure the guitar works mechanically. Plug it into an amp. Without strumming, there should be very little to no humming or buzzing. Note: If you are standing near a neon sign (which some guitar shops happen to have), the guitar will buzz loudly. To make sure the buzz is just the neon sign and not the guitar, turn away from the sign and the buzzing should get quieter. If it doesn't, the guitar itself is messed up.

9 Strum the guitar. You should be able to hear it clearly. The strings should not be hitting the neck or frets.

10 Turn up the volume on the guitar. It should get louder as you turn. Turn all the knobs and flip any switches on the guitar. They shouldn't crackle when you adjust them.

11 Gently wiggle the cord and move around a little. It shouldn't crackle or cut out, and the cord should stay tightly plugged into the guitar.

If you are buying a guitar or bass, you should expect there to be a li'l teeny bit of hum or crackle. More than a little bit is unacceptable. Also bad news: loud buzzing or rattling of any sort. If there is crackling when you turn the knobs, it's because the pots are dusty, and it's okay to ask the shop to clean them for you—but do this only if you are actually going to buy that guitar.

WHERE TO BUY GEAR AND WHERE TO STAY THE HECK AWAY FROM

I've bought guitars almost every way you can buy a guitar—from little shops, Guitar Center, garage sales, and

BUYING USED VS. BUYING NEW

The standard first buyers' guitars are the Fender Squier and the Epiphone Junior, which cost around $100 each. Daisy Rock, Dean, and Ibanez are brands with a couple of different types of beginner guitars for under $200. New guitars have a one- to five-year warranty, but nicer ones may come with a lifetime warranty. A warranty is important: It means that if something in your guitar is defective or fries out, the guitar company pays for it to be fixed—not you. At Guitar Center, used starter guitars are only $20 to $30 less than the brand-new versions, and you'll still have to pay a little extra for a warranty—so buying used can cost the same as new.

With a used guitar, there are the same advantages and problems as when you buy anything secondhand. It might be a deal, but you can't return it to the garage sale where you got it if it's defective. If you are buying used, get it from a source you can trust—a store, a friend, a friend of a friend, your neighbor's sister—someone who is not likely to sell you something that's half broken.

friends. I actually got my favorite guitar by trading someone a tape recorder and a haircut. There isn't a single best way or best place to get gear, but there are definitely some good ways and no-ways.

Little independent equipment stores depend on repeat business and keeping a good reputation, so the last thing these shops want is to sell you a bad guitar. There you can find new and used guitars that are in good shape and get help from a salesperson who can really help you find the right guitar, rather than try and sell you as much stuff as you can carry out of the store. Independent stores often have in-store repair, where they can set up (intonate and tune up) your guitar, and may offer lessons. The downside is that they may have a limited selection (rather than dozens and dozens of guitars, like in a chain store)—but they do often have beginner

THE OTHER GUITAR STUFF YOU NEED

☐ Strap

☐ Picks

☐ Tuner

☐ Set of strings

☐ Cable (10–15 feet)

deals on all the equipment you need to get started.

Guitar Center, Sam Ash, and other national chains are also good places to start since they carry a big selection of beginner guitars. You can try out a bunch and see what you like. They always have beginner's package deals, where you get a whole setup (guitar, amp, case, strap, and cable) for one price. Another advantage is that they carry everything you'll need, and they're usually cheaper than any other store around.

Buying equipment on eBay is not a smart idea until you know a lot about gear—it's too easy to wind up with junk. Getting gear through Craigslist or ads is a better bet, but still you have to know what to look out for—only do this if you have someone who really knows guitars and gear helping you shop. You *can* buy gear at a pawnshop, but that's kind of like going to a library to buy a hammer. A pawnshop is not in the music equipment business. Sure, they sell amps and saxophones, but they also sell pearl necklaces and power drills. The people working there may not know about the instruments they are selling; they might not know whether it works properly or if it's the right guitar for you. Ads, eBay, and pawnshops are methods for experienced players and buyers, which you will be in a few years, but it's not where you should start.

Wal-Mart, Target, and warehouse stores like Kohl's or Sam's Club also often carry guitars and other musical equipment for cheap. Some of the instruments they sell are toys, however, so just make sure you know the difference—and that you're getting something that's suitable for playing in a band. If you're not sure, ask—and if there aren't any experts on the scene (not too likely in a nonspecialty store), check where the guitar was made. Most major brands have a couple of different levels of quality that can be judged by where an instrument was manufactured. If it's from Mexico or Asia, it's generally of a lesser quality. If it's made in America, it'll have better electronics and wood.

DRUMS

With drums, what you see is what you get, so it's simpler than buying other instruments—you just have to know what it is you're seeing. There are a few things you want to look out for.

YOUR DRUM SET

ride cymbal

crash cymbal

rack tom

hi-hat

cymbal mount

snare drum

floor tom

stands, aka hardware

kick drum

1 Make sure the drum is not "out of round." It's essential that there are no warps or dents. To check if a drum is out of round, look at it and feel it, inside and out. You are looking for cracks, bulges, or any misshapen parts.

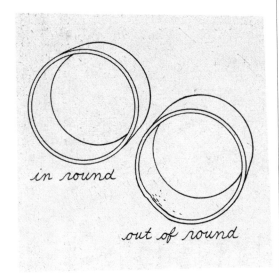

in round

out of round

2 Take the hoops and the heads off, and make sure the rim looks clean and round. There shouldn't be any nicks in the inside rim or warps in its shape.

3 Check out the hardware. The hardware refers to all the metal parts on the kit (on the drums, stands, pedals, and throne). The legs should fold out and be sturdy, the tension rods should screw and unscrew easily, and the hardware should be firmly attached to the drums. The aluminum rims should not be bent.

4 Cymbals shouldn't have any cracks in them. Cracks will only get worse. Most new cymbals come with a one-year warranty, so if you do split one in the course of normal play (i.e., you aren't hitting it with a hammer), you can get it replaced.

Most modern snare drums have eight or ten lugs; older ones might have six. With an eight- or ten-lug snare, you can have more balance and control in your snare, and it will stay in tune longer. The fewer lugs you have, the easier it is for it to go out of tune, and the more hassle the drum is going to be. Buying drums can get expensive fast, but the things that are worth spending a little extra on are a snare, a kick pedal, and a nicely padded drum throne. You are going to spend a lot of time on that little seat, so don't think you can get away with just using a kitchen stool or something. Yeah, sure, you *can* use a kitchen stool or regular chair, but

YOUR SNARE DRUM

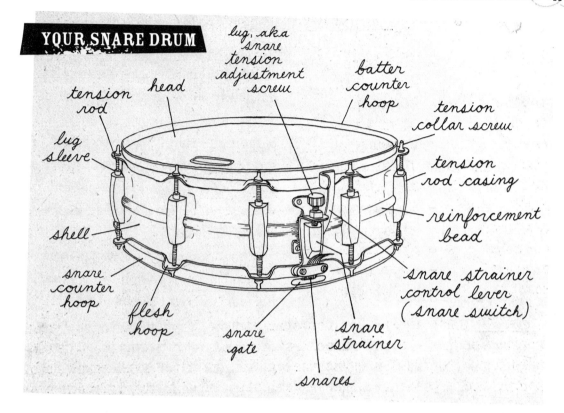

lug, aka snare tension adjustment screw

tension rod

head

batter counter hoop

tension collar screw

lug sleeve

tension rod casing

reinforcement bead

shell

snare strainer control lever (snare switch)

snare counter hoop

flesh hoop

snare gate

snare strainer

snares

it'll be the wrong height, you'll get weird bruises, and your butt will be in pain.

For your first kit, you can go either new or used. An entire drum kit and accessories bought brand new can easily cost $800. Buying a used kit that's in good shape is perfectly fine and it'll cost you half that. Older used kits are sometimes made of deader-sounding wood, but, basically, drums are what you make of them. With new drumheads and some patient tuning, almost any kit can sound awesome—so don't blow your life savings by buying the ultimate kit, brand new, today. Once you've been playing for a while, you'll have a better idea of what sort of sound or style you want. Then you can add or remove drums from your kit to work it out in whatever way sounds best. But whether you get a used or new kit, if you take care of it, you can play it for the rest of your life.

IT'S ALL IN YOUR HEAD

Drumheads (see diagram, page 11) help bring out different characteristics in your drum's sound, but they do not define how your drums sound. Drums sound like themselves. Old drums ring out less and new drums are usually louder and sustain more; drumheads will control this only to a certain point.

White drumheads can be single ply or double ply. Single ply are called "coated" and are what most people use on the top of the snare drum. They have a bright sort of pop to them. If you want a warmer drum sound or want the sort of sound you hear on '60s girl group records, these are the way to go.

Clear drumheads have a fatter, more resonant, boomier sound. Two-ply clear heads are the rock band standard.

Unfortunately, you'll find that no drumheads will make your drums sound like they do on your favorite records. In the studio, producers use "studio magic" to change how drums sound, and it's hard to replicate with an actual, real-life, drum kit.

DRUMSTICKS

When you first start drumming, you may have to go through a few different styles of sticks before you find the ones you are most comfortable with.

Drumsticks come in many sizes: 7a (thinnest, lightest), 5a (middle weight), 5b (heavier), and 2b (thicker

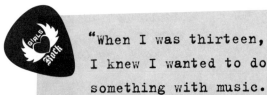

"When I was thirteen, I knew I wanted to do something with music. I saved up my money, bought a set of drums and realized that I didn't need to take lessons to play. What I would do is put headphones on and play along with a record. It felt really natural. It just was the easiest instrument to play, and I've never taken lessons."

GINA SCHOCK, THE GO-GO'S

THE OTHER DRUM STUFF YOU NEED AND DON'T NEED

NEED:

☐ **Drum key** (for tuning)

☐ **Sticks** (two pair)

DON'T NEED:

☐ **Cases.** Unless you are going on tour, drum cases just take up space. If you are just playing shows around town, it's fine to have your drums ride naked in the car, or wrapped in an old blanket, with your hardware in a big duffel bag.

☐ **Double-brace hardware.** Even if you are a totally sick heavy hitter in a thrash metal band, regular,

lightweight single-brace cymbal stands will be fine.

☐ **A gong.** The exception being that you should get a gong if you really want one, or if you start a gamelan orchestra instead of a rock band.

☐ **More than three cymbals.** A crash, a ride, and a hi-hat are all you need to begin.

☐ **A double-kick pedal.** Begin with one kick and one kick only. Once you have mastered that, you can move on. If you start with a double, you'll learn wrong and it'll mess you up forever.

and heavier) are some examples. The 5a and 5b are the most popular and are standard across brands.

Sticks are usually made from one of three types of wood. Maple sticks are good to start with because they are lightweight and have a little bit of flexibility to them. Hickory is the most commonly used, and it's a little bit heavier

and less flexible than maple. Oak is the most dense, heaviest, and least flexible, so you will feel the sticks' vibrations on your hands more when you play.

Sticks come with either wooden or plastic tips. There is not much difference, except plastic sounds a bit different on the cymbals, and wooden tips tend to last longer.

When you are buying a pair of sticks, weigh them in your hands—one shouldn't feel heavier than the other.

AMPS

Buying an amp is pretty simple, as there are only two things you have to consider: How loud do you need to be? Where and with whom are you playing? A small practice amp is perfect for playing in your bedroom but is no match for being heard over a drum set. If you know you are going to start a band and play shows, you should start with

PROTECT YOUR EARS!

Your hearing is what your entire future in music depends on, so you need to protect it. If you are playing in an amplified rock band, going to concerts, practicing loud on your own—you need to have plugs in your ears. Don't use toilet paper; it doesn't block out the frequencies that will mess up your hearing. Some of my friends who've played in bands since they were teenagers rarely wore earplugs; now, after a million practices and shows, they have a constant ringing in their ears (tinnitus). They talk louder than everyone else, and they constantly have to turn up their amps when they are playing.

Tinnitus is when you hear a high-pitched whistling, a roaring, whooshing sound, or a hum even though nothing around you is making that sound. It's common to hear it immediately after you've been at a concert or band practice without using earplugs. It is the direct result of being exposed to loud noises, and it signals that you have just damaged your hearing. Even though the ringing sound can come and go, the hearing loss is permanent. I have tinnitus, and, thankfully, I hear it only occasionally when I'm lying down to sleep, but it's loud, like someone's running a vacuum on my bed.

Custom-made plugs (which you can order off the Internet) are much better than regular foam earplugs. You or an audiologist uses a little kit to make an impression of your ears and you send it to the earplug maker and they send you back the fancy, heavy-duty earplugs that fit your ears perfectly. There are kinds made specially for performing musicians that filter out a lot of noise and frequencies so that you can still hear what's being played around you. These cost $100 to $150, but as long as you don't lose them, they'll last you forever. Save up, ask for a pair for your birthday—do what you have to do—*just get a pair.* Plus, if you ask your parents to help you buy an amp

or drums, they may be all "whatever," but if you ask them about custom earplugs, they'll probably say yes.

Good earplugs are as important as any other gear you want. If you don't have your hearing, making music isn't going to be your career, or even your hobby.

The Who guitarist Pete Townshend is famous for writing "My Generation"—and also for his hearing loss.

something bigger than a practice amp. You can always turn a bigger amp down, but with a little amp, you have a loudness limit. Some practice amps come with a headphone jack, so you can practice anytime and not bother anyone with the noise. They may also come with two inputs, which are useful if you want to plug in your iPod and play along to it, or if you have a friend over to play, you can both plug in.

There are four types of amplifiers—tube, solid-state, hybrid, and digital. Tube amps are the traditional, familiar sound of rock 'n' roll—warm, smooth, with a natural kind of distortion. The only problem is that the tubes are like little lightbulbs so you have to handle the amps with care to make sure they don't get rattled around or that the tubes don't get too hot. A tube amp can be temperamental, and you'll have to replace the tubes occasionally, but the minor hassle is worth it. When you are shopping for a tube amp, ask how often you'll need to replace the tubes and how much they cost, since it varies from brand to brand. Even if you play

a couple of hours every day, at most you'll have to replace them every six to twelve months.

Solid-state amps aren't as "rock" as tube amps, but they're durable and more practical than all the others; you can use them for anything and everything. You can sing out of them, and use them for keyboards, bass, or guitar. They have a clean, basic sound, and are cheaper than tube amps. You will never need to get a solid-state repaired unless it encounters a freak accident. Most keyboard amps are solid-state, and so are most bass combo amps and acoustic guitar amps.

Hybrids are solid-state amps with a tube pre-amp, so they have the warm sound of the tube with the durability of the solid-state.

Digital or modeling amps use software that imitates a couple of different guitar sounds or effects, so that rather than having a bunch of pedals, amps, and guitars, you just turn the dial on the amp to "heavy metal," "insane," or "tremolo" and there it is. Some people look down on that, like it's cheating, since there is a more classic, old-school

YOUR AMPS

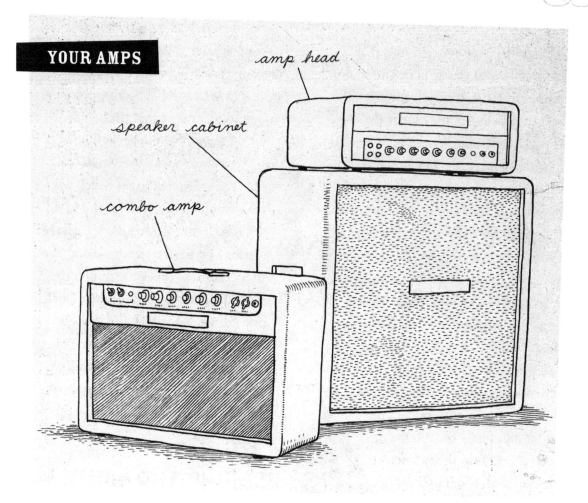

amp head

speaker cabinet

combo amp

way to get these sounds. Digital amps are popular with new-school metal bands, and they have an uncool rep, but they are not that bad—they're like the socially awkward, super-smart cousin of the other amps.

A LITTLE BIT ABOUT AMPS

There are two different types of amp setups: the combo amp and the head and cabinet. (See above.)

A combo has the amplifier guts (pre-amp and power amp) and the speakers in one box. Combos tend to be quieter and smaller, and have a sound that is associated with classic pop. The size of the speaker affects how it sounds—the bigger the speaker, the louder the amp. If you are playing places bigger than a coffee shop, small club, or a house show, the sound person is going to have to mic your combo amp and put it through the P.A., so that it is loud enough for everyone to hear it. Practice amps are combo amps.

A head and cabinet setup is two-piece: the amp head, which controls the power and the sound, and the cabinet, which is just a speaker that broadcasts whatever sound comes out of the head. You connect the guitar into the head, and the head connects to the cabinet, or "cab," which will usually be one, two, or four speakers. The amp head's wattage determines the intensity and loudness. Tube watts are much louder than solid-state watts (a 28-watt tube amp is about equal to a 100-watt solid-state amp). A 25-watt tube amp or a 50- to 100-watt solid-state amp will be enough to make sure that the people all the way in the back row can hear you. I used to have a Peavey RoadMaster, which was a fabulous 160-watt head, but it was so loud that I couldn't turn the volume up past "2" at shows for fear that I'd deafen the entire audience. Most people start with little practice amps or whatever low-end models they can afford. As you upgrade your gear and learn what sort of sound you want and what gear you need to achieve it, you'll eventually move on to bigger amps.

PICKING THE RIGHT INSTRUMENT

If you have already gone so far as to buy this book, chances are that you have a precise idea of the sort of band you want and what role you're going to play in it. If you don't—and you're just generally psyched about starting a band—there are a couple things that might help you along the path to your *destiny*.

1 If you already play one instrument, you are primed for another. If you play piano, switching to drums is a natural transition—they are both rhythm instruments. If you play a string instrument, learning bass or guitar should come naturally.

2 What instrument is available to you? Does someone in your family have an old guitar stashed away? Is there half a drum set on sale at the thrift store? Have you recently fished a xylophone out of your neighbor's trash? Scrounge around and snatch up what you can.

3 What instrument does your favorite person in your favorite band play? If you think Taylor Swift's the best, grab the nearest guitar and start practicing. Inspiration can go a long way.

4 Play whatever instrument your friend doesn't. If your friend plays bass or drums, try picking up the guitar. That way you can start a band together.

PROPER CARE AND FEEDING

Caring for your instrument is not terribly complex, but it's very important because it affects how the instrument sounds and how well it plays.

GUITAR/BASS

Don't drop it. Guitars are big, heavy, and durable, so it's unlikely they will shatter, but you can wind up with a chipped body or a bent neck, or all kinds of smaller issues. If you don't have a guitar stand (a good idea, but not mandatory), lay your guitar back in its case rather than leaning it against things, where it can fall or be tripped over.

Get a proper case. Most guitars come with a case of some sort; beginner models often come in a soft case called a gig bag. A gig bag is a lightly padded case that zips up and has straps and handles that make it easy to carry; it's useful if you are carrying your guitar around from place to place, or have to take the bus to your weekly lesson. It's lighter and less cumbersome than a hard case. The only problem is that it's more like a giant purse than a case. Your guitar will get jostled and will have to be tuned after riding around in there. A gig bag is suitable protection against hazards like drive-by eggings, dust, or a stiff breeze. (There are fancier/pricier gig bags that are almost as sturdy as a regular hard case, if you want the protection of a hard case without the clunkiness.) With a hard case, the guitar fits snuggly into a wood and fake fur interior, so even if it goes sailing down a flight of stairs, it'll live.

If you are going on tour, you must get a proper hard case. They are a pain in the butt to lug around, but doing so will toughen you up. If it's too much to carry on your own, ask a friend to be your roadie (that's what roadies do—carry stuff around). When you're carrying it, keep the lid facing your leg, so if it pops open, it'll hit your leg, rather than dump the guitar onto the floor.

Keep it in its case. It may look rad on display in your room, but it's an instrument, not a trophy or an objet d'art. When it's not in its case, it's more likely to get wet, dirty, chewed on by a pet, and touched by people who shouldn't be

YOUR BASS

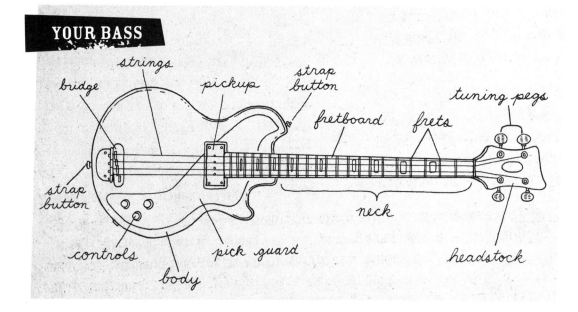

strings · bridge · pickups · strap button · fretboard · frets · tuning pegs · strap button · neck · controls · pick guard · body · headstock

touching your stuff. Do not keep it leaned against a wall, since that will warp its neck. If you want to look at your guitar all the time, take a picture of it and hang it next to your bed.

Keep it properly tuned. Tuning a guitar too high can also warp the neck.

Avoid extremes. Unless you are playing a plastic or metal guitar (lucky you!), your guitar is made of wood, and wood is vulnerable to the weather. If it's humid, it expands; if it's hot and dry, the wood dries out. Do not keep it in direct sunlight, the trunk of a car, or some other place it can get super hot or cold; do not keep it outside; do not expose it directly to rain or snow or hail or frost. Do not use it to serve food at your birthday party. Do not leave it unattended in a hammock overnight. Do not store it in your bathroom, garage, or attic. Do not keep it next to a radiator. Do not try and see if it floats. And do not store it in your basement if your basement is a damp place. (If you do not know if it's damp or prone to flooding, ask the adult who owns the basement.) A good place to keep a guitar when it is not in use is in a case under your bed or in a closet.

Keep it clean. Because you are touching it all the time, sweat and grime and little particles of skin (yuck) are going to get on the body, strings, and neck. Over time, this can make your guitar a bit gross. Use a cotton T-shirt or a clean cotton rag to polish it from time to time, but don't use a paper towel. Some people clean their guitar every time they play. I think that's unnecessary unless you sweat like a horse every time you touch the thing. Don't use any kind of cleaner unless it is specifically labeled as guitar polish. Otherwise, you

HIT THE BOOKS:
WOMEN WHO ROCK

Start stocking your shelves with rocking girl stories! Here are ten books about female rockers across musical genres and eras to put on reserve at your local library.

The Importance of Music to Girls by Lavinia Greenlaw (Farrar, Straus and Giroux, 2008). A truly inspiring book about loving music, this is a memoir of discovering music and growing up in England in the '70s, moving from glam to disco to punk.

Girls Like Us: Carole King, Joni Mitchell, Carly Simon—and the Journey of a Generation by Sheila Weller (Atria, 2008). Interwoven biographies of three great women whose music defined the '70s that makes for a really great and kind of gossipy read.

Be My Baby: How I Survived Mascara, Miniskirts, and Madness, or My Life as a Fabulous Ronette by Ronnie Spector and Vince Waldron (Onyx, 2004). A girl group pioneer dishes about her musical career and personal life.

Dirty Blonde: The Diaries of Courtney Love by Courtney Love (Faber & Faber, 2007). Photos, report cards, gossip, and more of the alt-rock queen's wit and wisdom.

Tori Amos: Piece by Piece by Tori Amos and Ann Powers (Broadway Books, 2006). The story of Tori!

should be fine just rubbing it with a rag. Clean the fret board before you put on a new set of strings to remove any gunk around the frets. If you want to keep your guitar pristine, you can get guitar polish at the guitar store.

Change your strings. It's a common beginner's misconception that strings last a long time. I kept my first set of strings on my guitar for almost a year, and they

I, Tina by Tina Turner, with Kurt Loder (Avon Books, 1987). Harrowing but ultimately redeeming classic autobiography.

Scars of Sweet Paradise: The Life and Times of Janis Joplin by Alice Echols (Holt, 2000). One of the great girl rock stars in all her excess and glory, with a lot about the '60s and the culture around her.

Janis Joplin

Petal Pusher: A Rock 'n' Roll Cinderella Story by Laurie Lindeen (Washington Square Press, 2008). The guitarist for Zuzu's Petals recounts the joy of being young and starting a band with her girlfriends.

Includes funny tour stories, romance, and adventure in a van.

Babes in Toyland: The Making and Selling of a Rock and Roll Band by Neal Karlen (Avon Books, 1995). What happens when an iconic female punk band tries to make it on a major label? Features cameos from the major figures of '90s alt-rock, (Nirvana, Sonic Youth), some gossip, and (bonus!) an unflattering picture of me when I was fifteen.

Early Work 1970–1979 by Patti Smith (W. W. Norton, 1995). Lots of times great rock lyricists get called poets, but in Patti Smith's case, she actually was one. This collects all her best work. Pure fire and page-shredding genius.

---

just got quieter and looser. If you play an hour or less every day, you should change strings every month or two. If you are playing several hours a day, you should change your strings every two weeks.

Wipe down the strings after you play a show or if you have had a long and sweaty practice. If you see any rust spots, change the strings. Over time you will be able to tell when your strings are "dead."

STRING THEORY

Guitar and bass strings get worn out the more you play them, and sometimes snap and break, so you will need to learn how to restring your guitar. Your guitar teacher or the folks at the guitar shop can explain. You'll know your strings are worn out when they start to sound really "dead" or "flat" (dull, and not bright and clear), or when they get to feeling gunked up or rusty.

Electric and acoustic guitars use similar kinds of strings, but not the same, so you have to use electric guitar strings on an electric guitar, and acoustic on acoustic. Most electric strings are some type of steel, with the lower three strings wound with nickel; most acoustic strings are steel, with the lower four strings wound in a bronze alloy. Both come in packs, and are packaged according to "gauge"—meaning according to the diameter, in inches, of the high E string.

Most people play nickel-wound "nines" or "tens" (string sets with high Es with a diameter of .009 inches or .010

Cindy Blackman, who plays drums with Lenny Kravitz, got her first drum kit when she was seven.

inches), but there are extra-light sets of "eights" and heavier sets of "elevens" and "twelves" available too. Start with a standard set of nines or tens. Most guitar stores sell individual strings, and it's good to get a few extra high E and B strings, since they tend to break more often.

It's important to put the right gauge strings on your guitar. What gauge you go with is up to you, but you may be limited by your guitar (short scale guitars generally use only lighter gauge strings). If you have your new guitar set up with tens when you buy it, and you break a string, be sure to restring only with tens; the wrong gauge strings will either be too close to or too far from the fret board, and will make your guitar unplayable. If you're unclear about what gauge string you should be using, ask the people at the shop where you got your guitar.

DRUMS

Avoid extreme temperatures. Don't keep your drums in the garage when it's cold or the trunk of a car on a hot day. They should be kept indoors, preferably someplace where the temperature doesn't fluctuate much, and where it isn't damp.

Oil them. Spray some WD-40 on the hinges of your kick pedal and other moving parts on your hi-hat stand from time to time.

Dust them if you feel like it. There really isn't much to do in terms of maintaining your drums beyond what's mentioned above.

CYMBALS

Let them warm up. If your cymbals have been in a cold place for any period of time, let them get to room temperature before you play them (or else they might crack). Once they are no longer cold to the touch, you can use them.

Keep them loose on the mounts. If your cymbals are tightened down too hard on their mounts (where they rest on top of their stands), they can't move freely. If you hit them while they are too tight, they can crack.

Protect your bell hole. You should always have a little felt ring and plastic protector on your mounts so that the bell hole on the cymbal doesn't hit the metal on the mount. If you don't, it'll not only sound bad, but it'll make the hole larger and eventually ruin the cymbal.

Don't let them get rusty. If you get sweat all over them, wipe them down. You can use a little steel wool on rust spots when they show, but don't rub too hard and don't use a power sander.

GUITARS—ALL KINDS!

One of the defining elements of rock 'n' roll is the electric guitar. The End.

Okay, actually, there are a slew of different types and brands. Here's a little overview to guide you in your buying and also to spur on your gear lust.

Kim Deal of The Breeders rocking her stratocaster.

ELECTRIC GUITARS

The rich history and evolution of rock 'n' roll revolves around the electric guitar in particular. From Fender to Gibson to Gretsch to Daisy Rock. Here are the basics you should know.

FENDER

The defining characteristic of all Fender guitars is that they have bolt-on necks. Bolt-on necks are attached to the body of the guitar with screws rather than glue, which gives them a unique style of sustain.

Stratocaster—Jimi Hendrix made this guitar popular. It has multiple tone knobs and three single coil pickups, so you can adjust them and get a variation of sounds from the guitar. Used by: Hendrix, Eric Clapton, Kim Gordon of Sonic Youth.

Jazzmaster—First produced in 1958, they were cheap and popular with punk bands, and came back into popularity in the '90s. They have a springy sound. The quintessential indie rock guitar. Used by: Elvis Costello, Thurston Moore of Sonic Youth, J. Mascis of Dinosaur Jr., and Mary Hansen of Stereolab.

Mustang—This was Fender's cheap student model; its bright tone made it popular as a rhythm guitar. They were discontinued and then repopularized in the '90s because Kurt Cobain of Nirvana played one. They're a short-scale guitar—shorter than a full-scale guitar but not as short as a three-quarter scale. Because of their size and cheap pickups, they have a thinner sound that is particular to Mustangs. People also like them because they look cool. Used by: Todd Rundgren, Heather McEntire of Bellafea.

Jaguar—Another shorter-scale guitar. They are brighter and more choppy and percussive sounding; they are really good as rhythm guitars. They have a certain twang to them that made them popular with '60s surf bands. Now they're popular with punk and alternative bands. Used by: Kurt Cobain, John Frusciante of the Red Hot Chili Peppers.

Telecaster—A brighter sounding, simpler guitar with two single coil pickups. Used by: Prince, Keith Richards of the Rolling Stones, Avril Lavigne, Merle Haggard.

GIBSON

Les Paul—Les Paul was a virtuoso jazz guitarist who pioneered the early rock 'n' roll sound, and made his first electric guitar from one big piece of wood. The model that bears his name has a full strong sound and is made from solid mahogany, with a maple cap on the body and an ebony fret board—which is a lot of heavy wood. Used by: Jimmy Page of Led Zeppelin, Corin Tucker of Sleater-Kinney, Slash of Guns N' Roses.

Corin Tucker of Sleater-Kinney with her Les Paul.

SG—A similar sound to the Les Paul but not as heavy. Famously associated with Angus Young of AC/DC, this is the guitar for loud rock. Used by: Gillian Gilbert of New Order, Carrie Brownstein from Sleater-Kinney, Pete Townshend of The Who.

Melody Maker—Originally, Melody Makers were Gibson's more affordable student guitars because they have a slightly shorter scale. They have a meaty, real rock 'n' roll sound that's a little snarly and not as full-sounding as a Les Paul. Played by Brian Bell of Weezer, Mick Jones of The Clash, and Joan Jett, who came out with her own signature model Melody Maker in 2008.

ES335—A semi-hollow body guitar, these were big in the early days of rock and used by dudes like Chuck Berry and B. B. King. They have a full, resonant tone, especially in the low end.

OTHERS
Rickenbacker—A favorite for singer/songwriters, they have a bright, jangly sound that made them popular as a

"If I wanted to be an astronaut, I could be an astronaut. If I wanted to be a doctor, I could do that. So, it never entered my mind that I couldn't play guitar. There's no rule that says girls can't play guitar."

JOAN JETT

rhythm guitar. Used by: Paul Weller of The Jam, Tom Petty, and John Lennon. They also make the definitive twelve-string guitar used by R.E.M., Johnny Marr of The Smiths, the Byrds.

Gretsch—Another classic maker of solid and hollow body electric guitars. They've got a full tone with some twang to it. Popularized by Chet Atkins. Used by: Billy Zoom of X, Elliot Easton of The Cars, George Harrison of The Beatles.

Jackson—Jacksons are for playing aggressive metal. They have multiple pickups for a clear, sharp lead tone—which is ideal when you are shredding and soloing nonstop.

Hamers—A favorite of metal bands and shredders, but they also make some rad Gibson-style guitars. Used by: James Honeyman-Scott of the Pretenders, Rick Nielson of Cheap Trick.

Silvertone/Airline—In the '60s and '70s, Silvertones were manufactured for Sears and Airlines for Montgomery Ward.

Most Hamers have a single neck but in this case, five is the charm for Cheap Trick's Rick Nielson.

Cheap starter guitars with a thin, bright tone, they were popular punk guitars in the '70s, and are still used by tons of garage and punk bands.

Supro/National—Cheapy guitars from the '50s and '60s. Supros (like Airlines) were sometimes made of Res-O-Glas, which is like plastic, which gives them a distinctive tone. They have a hollow sound that when it's distorted and dialed up has a slidey blues feel. Original vintage Supros are pricey, but Eastwood makes cheaper, reissue models. Jack White from The White Stripes plays Supros and Airlines, as does David Bowie.

Daisy Rock—Daisy Rock guitars are relatively new to the market; the company was founded in 2000. Targeted specifically to female players (both in size and design), Daisy Rock guitars are lightweight, and feature slimmer, "set" necks. The Debutante line (the younger sister to the traditional Daisy Rock line) has beginner guitars (fitting ages six to twelve), which are shorter scale and have bolt-on necks.

ACOUSTIC GUITARS

Though acoustic guitars were the precursors to electrics, and are quieter instruments, they are no less rocking.

Steel string—Used in country, blues, rock, and folk music. The size of the body determines the sound of the guitar. A bigger body will be louder, warmer, and more resonant. Smaller ones have a bright, percussive tone. Used by: Bright Eyes, Joni Mitchell, Neil Young, Kaki King.

Classical—Used in flamenco, classical, and indie rock. With a wider fret board, a mellow, round sound, and nylon strings instead of steel ones. Used by: Willie Nelson, Antonio Carlos Jobim.

PEDALS

Effects pedals are mostly used to alter the natural sound of guitars and basses. You can and should use them on whatever you want, though—even with

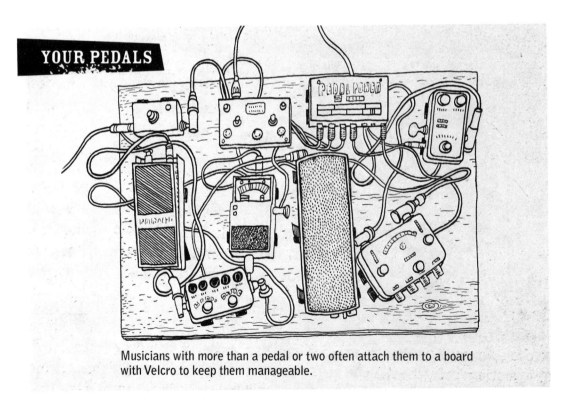

YOUR PEDALS

Musicians with more than a pedal or two often attach them to a board with Velcro to keep them manageable.

> "I think it's really cool to be so versatile. Part of what I want to do as a musician is incorporate everything I love about music into one thing. As long as it's genuine and passionate, I think it's cool if it's all over the map."
>
> **AMY LEE, EVANESCENCE**

keyboard or vocals. There is no instrument that isn't made better with an effects pedal or four. Being a pedal pig is a lot of fun, and you have a lot of options for your sound. Some of these pedals, especially vintage ones, can be pricey. Danelectro, though, makes a whole line of pedals that cost $15 each. If you want to expand your sound and try stuff out, that's a cheap way to start—and then work up from there.

DISTORTION

Distortion pedals are a girl's best friend. Distortion is the most classic and popular rock 'n' roll effect, and it's used in all styles of rock music from punk, to blues, to metal, and so on. There are three types of distortion; each will make your guitar sound bigger, more ragged, shreddier, and more aggressive.

Distortion—It's the most intense of the three types of distortion; it's the top level. The Rat pedal and the BOSS Distortion pedal are the most popular. Kim Gordon from Sonic Youth uses a Rat on her bass.

Fuzz—A step down from distortion. A fuzz pedal has a tight, synthetic, raspy, harsh, and focused sound. Its sound is a product of things in the circuit board being put together wrong, and was discovered by mistake. Fuzz pedals also compress the guitar sound a bit. The BOSS Fuzz is a favorite. Fuzz is good for a retro, '60s sound, and when used along with other pedals.

Overdrive—The mildest of the three, it simulates the sound of an overdriven amp. It pushes the sound, boosts it, and makes it edgier. The Ibanez Tube Screamer is the traditional favorite.

For distortion, you can also get an amp simulator pedal that has sounds that are based on popular amps (such as the Vox AC30, Marshall Stack, or Mesa Boogie). Because they simulate the sound of an amp, you can plug them directly into a mixer or your four-track (or whatever you record on). The Tech21 Sans Amp is a good one.

OTHER EFFECTS

Delay—Gives you a remote, echoey sound. Delay is the key component in the guitar sound for U2, The Cure, and Animal Collective.

Chorus—It gives things a small, shimmery sound. The effect is kind of dated and '80s-metal sounding. The breakdown on Metallica's "Master of Puppets" is chorus in action.

Flanger/Phase Shifters—Similar to chorus but more metallic, smoother, and rounded sounding. They have a wider range and affect the tone more drastically. They have a kind of jet swoosh sound (the monster flange jam: "Freak Scene" by Dinosaur Jr.). The Boss Flanger and the reissue Sovtek Small Stone phasers are popular favorites.

Compression—Used to even out the guitar tone so the bottom and top notes are equally loud. It mashes down the loud parts of the signal and pushes up the quiet parts. Compressors are useful if you play a lot of solos because they help make all the notes be heard, not just the higher, more piercing ones. They also add sustain and make the notes ring out a little longer. Compressors are good to pair with Rickenbacker, Jaguar, and Jazzmaster guitars, which don't otherwise have much in the way of sustain.

Reverb—Some amps have built-in reverb, but most of the time, you'll have to get a pedal to replicate the sound. The Electro-Harmonix Holy Grail is about $100, and though it's a digital pedal, it has a really natural reverb sound.

> "I'm not trying to reinvent anything. I'm not trying to change four players, boom, boom, boom, a couple notes, three chords."
>
> **CHRISSIE HYNDE, THE PRETENDERS**

Retro garage and surf bands use them. The alt-rock band Jesus and Mary Chain's wall-of-soft-fuzz sound is a combo of reverb and fuzz pedals.

Tremolo—Adds a choppy vibrato to your sound. The intro to The Smiths' "How Soon Is Now" (which you should definitely listen to whether you care about tremolo or not) is a tremolo pedal, as is "Crimson and Clover"; The White Stripes use it, too.

Pitch Shifter/Harmonizer/Octave Pedal— These pedals allow you to adjust your guitar sounds up or down an octave— most people go down. The Electro-Harmonix Pog pedal allows you to do both at the same time. This makes your guitar more bassy sounding and it's often used in bands where there is no bass (The White Stripes, Yeah Yeah Yeahs, for example) because it makes the guitar sound like it's also playing a bass part. It makes your guitar sound huge.

A harmonizer pedal allows you to harmonize to 4ths and 5ths—basically, if you play one note, it'll make a three-note harmony. DigiTech Whammy is a favorite. BOSS HR-2 Harmonist is a good one, and also sounds good on an organ. Harmonizers are used a lot in older metal; it can make it sound like you are doubling the lead guitar. Think Iron Maiden. Annie Clark of St.Vincent/Polyphonic Spree uses a Digitech Whammy.

Wah-Wah—A wah pedal is a movable filter, sort of like the mid-range control of an EQ, which lowers some frequencies and raises one "peak" frequency. When you move the pedal, it moves the peak frequency from low to high (and back). It causes a very vocal sound, a bit like a crying baby. It takes some practice and skill to master, since you don't just stomp on it; you adjust it as you play by moving your foot. Jimi Hendrix's "Voodoo Chile (Slight Return)" is *the* classic wah cut of all time. They're popular in psychedelic, blues, glam, and '70s metal bands. The Dunlop Cry Baby and the Vox Wah are popular models.

Envelope Filter—Makes a filter open and close around each note. It's basically an automatic wah pedal (sometimes called "auto-wah"). An essential, classic funk sound, used by the Red Hot Chili Peppers, Jerry Garcia of The Grateful Dead, and Bootsy Collins—Stevie Wonder used one on his clavinet on "Higher Ground"; The Who's "Going Mobile" uses it, too. The Mutron is the classic auto-wah.

Looper—Allows you to record a little segment as you play and, once triggered, it will repeat that part over and over. Some loop pedals slow and speed it up and reverse it. It can also be used on drums and vocals. Electro-Harmonix Memory Man, Line6, and Boss Loop Station are good, but loop pedals are generally kind of expensive—$200 to $300.

KEYS OPEN DOORS: KEYBOARDS IN A NUTSHELL

Most rock bands don't have keyboards, but they can add a lot to your band's sound. They can make things more melodic, rhythmic, atonal, freaked-out, and dramatic. Keys are frequently used on recordings, even when bands don't usually have a piano. Most studios have a piano, and they often wind up making an appearance.

I GOT IT FOR CHEAP: MINOR KEYS CAN BE MAJOR

At nearly every thrift store in America, there is a used, functioning Casio synthesizer keyboard languishing on a shelf. It probably costs between $4.99 and $30. It might be tiny and crappy and really '80s sounding. Actually, not "might"—*it will*. It is not going to sound like a real piano. If used correctly (or maybe incorrectly)

Keyboardist Stacy DuPree formed Eisley with her sisters; they put out their first major label record when she was fourteen.

you can create some really cool sounds, though. Cheap/crappy/old keyboards can turn awesome when run through a pedal or two (chorus, distortion, RAT) and hooked up to a guitar amp. You can customize or beef up a keyboard's plinky sound if you aren't into it. Using an amp made specifically for keyboards is unnecessary because when you play a live show, keyboards are often plugged directly into the P.A., so even if all you have is a teeny-tiny practice amp, your keyboard can still be cranked up and rocked out.

PIANOS

The funny thing about pianos is that, unlike the other popular rock instruments, they are not portable. *Yes*, technically portable, but they are not easily moved with fewer than three burly people and a freight elevator. It's just not feasible to load a piano into the back of a station wagon and get it to your gig, and then spend a couple of hours retuning it. It's just not happening. Pianos are *especially* special instruments because nothing duplicates the beauty and lusciousness of their sound.

> "I can't allow myself to be influenced by how I might be perceived by pop music or by anyone in terms of what I want to do as an artist. I can only go by how I perceive myself."
>
> **SINÉAD O'CONNOR**

You can get synthesizers that imitate it, but their "piano" settings are always a little artificial sounding. Using a real piano on recordings gives songs class and mood.

Grand piano—As the name suggests, it's giant and has an air of elegance; the kind of piano you think of when you think of a piano. Used by Elton John, Billy Joel, and Tori Amos.

Upright piano—Not as resonant as a grand, and not as frouffy. Upright is much more of a rock band standard. Used by The Band, Tom Waits, Radiohead, PJ Harvey, and nearly everyone who has ever made a record in a studio.

> "I love teaching myself things. In a way that handicaps me, because when someone tries to instruct me, I can't be instructed.... Someone will say, 'Oh, I like the way you play piano, will you play these key changes C to E?' And I can't do it. The only way I could is if they play the tapes and let me wander around and choose my own chords."
>
> **JONI MITCHELL**

ELECTRIC PIANOS

The difference between an electric piano and a regular piano is that, instead of keys hammering wires, there are little metal tines—kind of like on a fork—that vibrate and sound similar to a bell when the hammer hits them. The tines aren't as resonant and boomy as the long metal piano wire. Electric pianos tend to have fewer keys than the eighty-eight that regular pianos have.

Fender Rhodes—An electric piano with a smooth, soft, and sparkly tone that sounds a bit like a bell underwater. It came in several different setups (with seventy-three or eighty-eight keys), including a suitcase model. Used by Herbie Hancock on "Watermelon Man," Stacy DuPree of Eisley, Billy Preston on later Beatles records.

Wurlitzer—A similar sound to the Rhodes, but with a brighter tone with more bark to it. Used by Ray Charles on "What I Say," Panic at the Disco's "Mad as Rabbits."

Clavinet—A sixty-key electric piano closely associated with funk and reggae; each note makes a kind of *wAHw-wAHw* sound. Used by Stevie Wonder on "Superstition," Herbie Hancock's album *Headhunters*, Gorillaz's "Dirty Harry."

ORGANS

Organs are like pianos in that they have a foot pedal, but on the organ, the foot pedal just controls volume. Organs are not very touch sensitive, meaning you can't really play softly. It's kind of an off/on situation only. An organ will hold the note as long as you are playing it. Musicians use organs to shrink and swell parts of a song, so you use the volume pedal to tame the sound; otherwise, it just blurts. They also have a series of knobs called drawbars, which you push in or pull out to emphasize certain overtones; that way, you can make the sound brighter or dark or crispy. You use different tonalities in different parts of songs—if you are trying to fill up a song to give it some meat (Yo La Tengo's first five records), you want something dark, rich, full. If you are going to whip out a solo, you want something crispy, bright, with attack (The Doors' "Light My Fire"). You can sometimes find an organ for cheap or free on Craigslist, all you have to do is pick it up. Keep in mind that they are heavy and difficult to move—like pianos, organs aren't something you can cart off to a show, they are more for recording or at-home recitals.

Hammond—These are gigantic, monster organs with two decks of keyboards that synthesize the sound of horns, strings, and flutes. They don't sound particularly like real horns or strings, but you get the basic idea that that's what it's supposed to be. They have their own unique and very cool sound. The signature trilling sound of the popular Hammond B3 comes from its Leslie cabinet speaker. Inside the Leslie, two speakers rotate; when they whip around, it makes a tremulous, vibrating *wahwahwahwahwah* sound. It has two

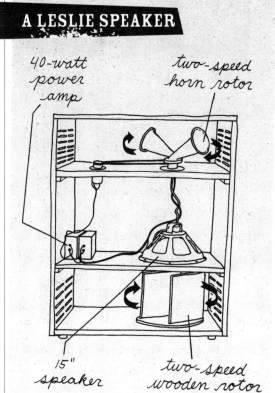

A LESLIE SPEAKER

40-watt power amp

two-speed horn rotor

15" speaker

two-speed wooden rotor

The chirpy Farfisa keyboard is the hallmark of the unique sound of The B-52's.

Farfisa and Vox Continental—These have a reedy sound to them that can be shrill, whiny, and insect-like. In high school, I was in a band with two Farfisas and it was like getting honked at by two ginormous geese—in a good way! Like the Rhodes and Wurlitzer, the Farfisa is easy to transport. You can unscrew the legs and fasten its lid on, and suddenly it's the world's heaviest suitcase. It's easy to go gig-to-gig with it. Farfisas have been used by the B-52's, Green Day, Led Zeppelin on "Dancing Days," and Pink Floyd on "Time." The Vox Continental was used on The Beatles' "I'm Down" and Elvis Costello's "Pump It Up."

Mellotrons and Chamberlins—These organs were precursors to synthesizers (see right). Each note, when pressed, plays a little repeating loop that sounds like a simulation of voice, horns, flute, or strings. Famously used by: The Beatles on the intro of "Strawberry Fields Forever," The Moody Blues on "Nights in White Satin," and The Flaming Lips on the *Yoshimi* album. Chamberlins also show up on David Bowie's *Heroes* and Fiona Apple's *When the Pawn . . .*

different speeds, slow and fast; when it's faster, it gives the sound more emphasis. The effect of the cabinet is to keep the organ from being an intense brick wall of sound; it breaks up its honkiness a bit. Hammonds are heavy and need three strong people to carry them.

Famously used by Pearl Jam, The Grateful Dead, Tori Amos on *The Beekeeper*. Booker T. and the MGs and Coldplay have also used Hammonds.

SYNTHESIZERS

Synthsesizers can replicate the sounds of an orchestra. Synths can produce the sounds of all the keyed instruments already mentioned, plus a ton of others (rain stick, viola, cowbell) all in one computer program. You'd never mistake a synthesizer's sound for the Chicago Symphony Orchestra, but synth horns and strings have their own unique fake quality that's beautiful and grand. You've got maximum options—think of how many sounds you get for the price of one!

Originally, synth keyboards came with only two sounds (or "patches"): bad organ and bad piano. Now, there are kinds where you can do different things to change the sounds they play, and they can sound great.

There are stand-alone analog synthesizers—Moog, Arp, and Oberheim are the best known—and each has their own spacey-computery sound qualities. They have knobs and buttons where you adjust the shape of the sound wave, the speed of oscillation (the wah-wah sound) and the shape of the filter. They're expensive, hard to find, and they play only one or two sounds, but still very, very rad.

YOUR VOICE

Your voice can be one of the most powerful instruments you ever own (if you choose to use it). And, it's free! Voice lessons, of course, can get pricey, but there are plenty of musicians who have never taken one in their lives—they just sing to express themselves and enjoy exploring the range of sounds they can achieve. Your voice does require special care, though, because when it gets strained, you can't just pick up some new guitar strings to fix it.

HOT FOR TEACHER

Now that you have your instrument, you can start learning to play. There is no one right way to learn; you can take lessons or teach yourself. Private lessons, classes, instructional books or DVDs, videos on YouTube, rock camp— explore your options to find what feels right and works best for you. When I first started playing guitar, I thought I *had to* take lessons, so I went to the guitar shop near my house and laid down $30 for three lessons. I assumed that the guys working at the shop were know-it-all wizards and could ably teach me anything and everything I needed to know. Instead, I sat in a basement room for a half hour watching a very frustrated, ancient dude try to teach me the lamest classic rock beginner tune of all time, "Smoke on the Water," a song I didn't know, and didn't want to know, from an era of music I hated. I never bothered with my third lesson.

The problem was twofold. One, the guitar teacher had a very set idea that there was only one way to learn and play. Secondly, I didn't do my research. If you want to start with lessons or a class, talk to the teacher beforehand. My teacher had never heard of any of the bands or music I was into, and when I brought him tapes of stuff I wanted to learn, he laughed at them (seriously!). Ask potential teachers about what styles they teach, and be upfront about what you want to learn—use the checklist on page 43 to guide you. You don't have to be best buds, but you want a good teacher who can teach you what you want to learn.

Lessons are a good way to learn the basics *properly*—so you don't have to unlearn a bad habit you picked up when you first started. A few years ago, I took bass lessons for two months in order to learn the songs of a band I was going to tour with. Even though I had been playing bass for ten years and it is the instrument that comes most naturally to me, it was really frustrating. I had never learned to play using my pinky, only my first three fingers. These bass lines required the use

of all four fingers, which meant hours of taming my pinky: playing scales, chords, and finger exercises—the stuff I had brushed off years earlier because it was boring and I thought I'd never need it.

Before you start taking lessons, think about what you want to get out of it. Do you want to learn how to read music? Do you want to learn the basics and then go on your own? Do you want help with a particular style of music? You have to know your basic goal(s); otherwise, all of the work you've put in is going to feel more like a hassle than your exciting first steps toward rock stardom. Even if your parents are forcing you to take lessons, at the very least, you will improve faster than you would playing on your own—unless you are a Mozart-style child prodigy, in which case you should put down this book and go compose a sonata.

That said, lessons or classes are not for everyone. Personally, I learn best from (or along with) my friends, and by playing in a band. Learning by doing can be just as good. Joining or starting a band means that you'll spend at least a couple of hours every week practicing and writing songs.

> "When you write songs, you can't really point out the exact thing you're inspired by. It's more a state or a mood or an atmosphere that you're trying to put into words."
>
> **—KEREN ANN**

Some people think that you have to learn how to be really good at an instrument before you can play in a band. That is a myth; you can start a band as soon as you want, as long as you can find people to play with. Maybe give yourself a day or three to play around with your instrument, but there is no law that says you can't have your first band practice twelve minutes after you get your drums home.

Being self-taught doesn't mean winging it on instinct alone. There is an ocean of how-to books, DVDs, and play-along CDs that are perfectly instructive. You can find them at the library or at instrument stores and bookstores. While how-to books are great (especially the one you're reading right now), you should combine your book learning with some DVDs, YouTube, or CDs, just to check your work and make sure you are getting it right. My friend and former bandmate Miles tried using a book when he got his first guitar at fourteen, and misunderstood some of the instructions on how to press on the strings. He spent his first few weeks wondering why the strings made a hideous buzzing noise instead of notes. He got a different book, one that was just illustrations of finger positions for chords, and figured it out.

There are a couple of reliable standby brands of instruction books. Mel Bay publishes tons of really easy to understand books that will teach you beginner bass or ultra-advanced banjo on up to funky African hand drumming. A lot of the books are paired with play-along CDs or DVDs, so you can hear right away if you are learning correctly. You can get those books at the music store, or order them online. Hal Leonard puts out a lot of instruction books, and also publishes the sheet music for everything from Broadway musicals to Fall Out Boy guitar parts, and

anything else you could want. If you are interested in music theory, improvisation, and learning jazz stuff, check out Jamey Aebersold (jazzbooks.com). They have a lot of play-along materials, summer music camps, and how-to horn stuff.

FINDING A TEACHER

Even if you live in the teeniest micro-small town, you can find someone to take lessons from. The world is filled with unemployed musicians who support themselves by teaching other would-be musicians. Check the bulletin board at the music shop; call a music school in your area or the music department at a nearby college. Ask your music teacher at school. Ask your neighbor's piano teacher. Ask any musician you know. Once you have some leads, consider this: If you are even half serious about your playing, and/or interested in music as a career, you should take lessons from someone who is a working musician. Some people who give lessons for a living and have spent the last seventeen years doing so have never stepped onstage to perform themselves. Professional instructors can teach you everything you'd ever want to know about playing, but someone who has experience playing in a band and recording will clue you in on a lot more and can be a great resource once you start your band. Here is a checklist for selecting a teacher:

1 Get a recommendation or talk to other students. Just because he or she is a great musician doesn't automatically make for a great teacher.

2 He or she should have experience teaching people your age. If your potential teacher has only taught adults, he or she might not be right for you.

3 He or she should have a couple of years of teaching experience. Everyone has to start somewhere, but it's better if the first lesson isn't a first for *both* of you.

4 Ask what styles he or she teaches. Ask this *before* telling him or her what style you are interested in learning.

5 How long are the lessons, and how much do they cost? Lessons should last 30 to 60 minutes. Cost will vary.

Hopefully, asking those questions has helped you find a teacher that is a good match for you. Here's a checklist of questions to ask yourself once you start working with the teacher:

Y	N	
—	—	Does she have a positive attitude?
—	—	Does she offer encouraging feedback?
—	—	Do you feel comfortable asking questions?
—	—	Does she build your confidence?
—	—	Does she build your skills?
—	—	Do you feel like you are really learning something?

It can take two or three lessons to settle in with a teacher, but past that, if you are not feeling it—if you are answering "no" to any of the questions above—*you don't have to stick with him or her.* A good teacher can change your life, but a bad one can make you want to give up.

CHAPTER 2

MAKING ☆ THE BAND ☆

I f you've decided that you aren't going solo, then it's time to get your band together. A band can be you and someone else (a duo), or ten of your closest friends. Most rock bands have between three and five people, so that there is a bassist, a guitarist, a drummer, and someone to sing. How big your lineup is depends on what kind of sound you want and how many people you need to achieve it. You can get by with two people—The White Stripes have a minimal lineup of just guitar and drums; Polyphonic Spree has twenty-three members, including a mini-choir.

BAND TOGETHER

N ow, *deciding* to start a band is the easy part, but forming one requires a little more work. If you don't already have some friends lined up, you'll have to put the word out. Tell everyone you know that you are trying to start a band. Tell your sister, your sister's friends, your sister's friend's brother, families you babysit for, your drum teacher, and your math teacher. You never know who's going to hook you up. Tell people at school who are obsessed with music—even if they aren't into the same music as you. If you are in high school, chances are there is a girl in your class who is a sick metal drummer and playing in a band she hates (this is a universal truth). You just have to find her. One of the people you tell may know her and introduce you.

Don't be discouraged if your family and friends aren't eager to play with you. Not everyone's social circle is a hotbed of musical talent. It's not unusual for bandmate searches to take a while. Be vigilant in your hunt and keep practicing and working on your ideas. I played in a band where we couldn't find a singer for over a year. We had a dozen people try out, including a guy who brought a little ceramic donkey with him for inspiration (that donkey did him no good—he sang like a sick cat). Still, we kept practicing and

practicing, singerless. One night, we went to a show and the opening band was a guy playing guitar and singing by himself. He kept making jokes that he was solo because he couldn't find anyone to be in a band with. He was a perfect fit for us, so after the show we accosted him and let him know he'd be joining our band. And he did—after we'd spent a year totally focused on our playing, we were a band worth joining.

If you have asked around, begged all your friends' friends and still can't find someone to play music with, you'll have to cast a wider net. There are a couple options:

1 Ask adult musicians you know. Tell your guitar teacher, the choir director at school, the woman who teaches your sister violin—that you are looking for someone your age to start a band with who plays drums, sings, etc.

2 Make a flyer and put it up on the bulletin board at your school/church/temple/store where you bought your amp. Make sure this is cool with your parents before you do it since you are inviting total strangers to contact you.

3 Contact the music school near you. Check on their website or call and find out if they have after-school or summer programs for students your age. Have your parents ask other parents about music programs or camps.

4 See if your city or park district offers classes. Community music programs sometimes have open mic performance nights for teens (where anyone can show up and perform)—a surefire way to hook up with other people who want to start a band.

5 Find out if there is a Girls' Rock Camp in your area. They might have suggestions, classes you can take, or a bulletin board where you can post a flyer (see pages 54 and 55).

START WHERE YOU ARE

Despite my previous story about holding out for the right bandmate, I'm going to give you some contrary advice: Play with whomever you can find—anyone who is eager to play and has an instrument. Even if he just started playing drums three days ago and couldn't find a beat if you handed it to him in a bag. Even if she's your cousin, the flute virtuoso, who loves all the emo bands you hate. You have to try it out, and this is why:

1. You will learn from the experience, even if it's frustrating or boring.

2. You never know who'll be your ideal musical partner.

3. Playing with people who are better musicians will make you a better musician.

4. Playing with people who are just learning is (usually) super fun because they have the weirdest ideas.

5. Collaborating with people who are into different music will expand your skills and give your band a more unique sound.

6. All practice is good practice.

Your first band isn't going to be the only band you ever start, so don't sweat it if it doesn't work out. The three-bassists-and-one-tambourine group that you spend the summer jamming with will help prepare you for the band of your dreams. As long as the people you are

> "The lightning bolt came out of the heavens and struck Ann and me the first time we saw The Beatles on *The Ed Sullivan Show* . . . that was the moment Ann and I heard the call to become rock musicians. I was seven or eight."
>
> **NANCY WILSON, HEART**

comes up with lyrics that make you want to stick your head in the toilet and flush.

BEST FRIENDS, BEST BANDMATES

An ideal band member is someone that you get along with personally and musically. You don't have to be BFFs, but you need to at least *feel* friendly in order to collaborate. Playing in a band with your friends can be super fun; being creative *together* can make you much closer. The other side to this is that being in a band involves ambition and expressing who you are, which can bring out a different side of someone that you've never seen.

When you write a song, you're taking personal ideas and making them public. There is risk in that. People may not like your songs. Those people might be your bandmates. You might spend two weeks writing a song that is the most heartfelt, intense art you've ever made. You bring it into practice, proud and hopeful, and play it for them and they tell you no way. It's too sappy. It's too fast. It sounds like a Pearl Jam song they hate. Your best

playing with aren't jerks and you aren't a jerk, then you'll have fun and learn how to collaborate, how to take everyone's little ideas and turn them into one big idea. Worst case scenario: It stinks and there's no musical chemistry, so you make a hasty exit. A fruitless afternoon spent jamming with your neighbor will help you figure out what you want in a band experience, and it will help you learn how to be in a band. You'll learn to explain your ideas to people, how to play along with other instruments and how to be polite and constructive when your singer friend/drummer may offer you some criticism on how to change a verse that you feel is perfect. You may feel inclined to throw a mic stand at her and storm out yelling, "I QUIT!"—don't.

Because this song is an expression of who you are, it can feel like she's rejecting or criticizing *you* rather than your song. It's natural that everyone's egos get tangled up, and that you might get in a fight over changing two notes in the chorus. Everyone is attached to their ideas, so all the little details start to feel super important.

This is the trickiest part when you are playing with other people. You want songs to be good, you want everyone to be happy, *and* you want to be free to express and create. You have to balance those interests, and there isn't always an easy way to do it. Sometimes, all you can really do is try not to take things personally, stand up for your ideas when they are truly important to you, and cooperate as best you can.

If you are forming a band with a good friend—especially someone whose friendship is essential to you—you have to have a talk before you play even a single note. Even if you've been best friends since you were three and have

The Runaways singer Cherie Curie and lead guitarist Lita Ford. They were teenagers when the band formed in 1975.

> "I'd like women to be part of a band because of their talent, not because it's cool to have a girl in the band. I can't stand the idea of a woman who just stands there looking pretty."
>
> **CHRISTINA SCABBIA, LACUNA COIL**

never had a fight, you *have* to have this talk: You must agree that you will always put your friendship first. Make a pact (a pinky swear or a solemn oath will do) to talk out any and all disagreements, and that whatever happens at practice stays at practice. Meaning, if you get mad because she refuses to turn down her amp, you have to deal with it right then, or talk it out after practice. You can't carry that annoyance with you to school the next day and slam your locker in her face or sit at lunch in silence. Fights and disagreements are part of being in a band—you can't avoid them. As long as you always make the effort to preserve your friendship, your band and friendship will be the better for it.

Being in bands with my best girlfriends helped me to have the courage to get onstage and show my ideas to the world (and by "the world" I mean all fourteen people who came to our shows). Though I'm not a shy person, I was petrified of being onstage. I was able to do it only because it wasn't just me up there, it was *us*. I turned around in between songs and made panicked faces indicating that I was pretty sure I was dying, or at least having a minor heart attack, and my friend leaned over her drums and said, "You are ruling it. Don't worry!" She might have been saying that just to make me feel better, but it gave me enough confidence to get through the next song. It was also great to be able to share our accomplishments and laugh off our miserable failures together; our band was like a family. Playing in a band with friends can make your band a better band because you want to impress them; you all want to be awesome *together*.

WILD COMBINATION: FINDING YOUR MATCH

Once you've found people to start a band with, there's some business to address before you get down to business. It needn't be the Spanish Inquisition, but there are some questions to ask to make sure everyone's on the same page.

★ **How often can your band members practice?** Twice a month? Every day after school?

★ **What other stuff do they have going on in the future—sports, camp, lessons, babysitting?** You don't want to start playing and discover that you can't practice for three months because your bass player made JV basketball. Make sure everyone has time to practice and has a way to get to practices.

★ **Discuss how long you've been playing.** You don't have to be at the same skill level in order to start a band. Playing with people who are more skilled musicians than you can be intimidating at first, but it'll teach you a lot. A good musician raises the skill level of everyone she plays with. Once you start playing with someone you'll find out pretty fast if they are cool with playing with a beginner. When I was in the tenth grade, I joined a band with some guys I didn't know very well, and at the second practice, the guitarist turned to me, all huffy, and said, "I thought you said you'd been playing bass for a year?!" I was totally mortified. It felt like I'd been punched in the gut. I actually *had* been playing for a year, but, unlike him, I was self-taught and didn't spend six hours a day practicing. Rather, I spent an hour or two goofing around and trying to play along with my favorite songs.

"We used to get a kick out of making people feel really uncomfortable. . . . Basically, our behavior was designed to horrify. You have to remember that girls behaving that badly were a real rarity at the time."

BELINDA CARLISLE, THE GO-GO'S

★ Be aware that every musician has a really different idea of what "good" playing is. If you're playing with people and they harsh on your skills, quit the band and forget them fast. Don't let it bum you out and don't *ever, ever, ever* waste time playing with people who bring you down or make you feel bad about the way you play. There are plenty of people out there who like playing with beginners and will appreciate your ideas and enthusiasm.

My first few months of playing bass in a band were with my friend and her neighbor—we'd started at the same time and had no idea what we were doing. We only knew two chords, had no idea how to tune our instruments, and my friend could only play her drums for about ten minutes before she felt completely exhausted. But none of that mattered to us—all that mattered was that we were playing music. Every ridiculous sound and rhythm was a dream coming true; we were making something out of nothing and that felt pretty genius to us. We knew it sounded terrible and would collapse in crying fits of laughter in between each song that we made up and promptly forgot. There is plenty of time ahead for you to be studied and serious; when you are a beginner, the main thing is to have a good time, all the time.

STYLE WARS

You and your potential bandmates have probably already talked about what kind of music you want to make since that's usually the first thing to come up. The next thing you need to do is exchange mixes with your potential future bandmate(s)—even if you have the same exact favorite bands. Burn a CD or post a mix online of your favorite songs that inspire you most. By checking out what the other person is into, you'll find the places where your tastes match up, which is better than listing off the contents of your iTunes.

Talk about what other instruments you'd like to have in the band, how intense or aggressive you'd like your sound to be, and how many people you think the band

Practice made perfect for the original shredder, Sister Rosetta Tharpe.

should have. None of this has to be set in stone, it's just to get an idea of each other's expectations for the band to make sure they are not wildly opposed.

One thing that you absolutely must agree on is how serious you're going to be about the band. If you just want a band to goof around with on weekends, say so. If you want to make records and go on tour, you have to be in a band with people with those same goals. Playing shows, recording, touring, or trying to turn your music into a career means devoting a lot of your free time to the band—nights, weekends, after school, all summer. If you're serious about music, you can't be in a band with someone who isn't—even if you're a perfect musical match. It's hard to keep a group together when half the band wants to practice every night and the other members don't want to bother. You don't want someone quitting the band right before a recording session or an important show because they don't want to put in the work.

This may seem like a lot to discuss before you officially begin your band, but it doesn't need to be a series of tense ultimatums ("If you can't practice weekends, it's OVER!"). It's just about sharing your ideas and making sure you are on the same page. Sure, rock is all about spontaneity and chemistry and feelin' it, but nothing is diminished by planning things out. You guys might decide to have a band for the summer because one of you is too busy to practice once school starts. Or you'll end up spending a weekend making a record in your bedroom because you aren't interested in having a full-time band and your friend is. There are a lot of solutions in between *band* and *no band*.

FLYER JARGON

If you are browsing ads in hopes of joining someone else's band, there is a phrase you will come across, usually in all caps: "PRO GEAR, PRO ATTITUDE A MUST." Any ad that says "PRO" something or other ("pro look" or "pro skills") means the band is probably a group of older guys in a metal cover band that plays weekly at a suburban dive bar. Having a "professional attitude" is really important—if you are a temp secretary, that is. Don't worry about having a professional attitude until you are playing the Verizon Wireless Music Center, or your band is paying for your college education, whichever comes first.

The term "gigging band" also comes up. This means the band plays locally, maybe even regionally. This is different than "touring band" which means playing strings of shows around the country or around the world. If a band is already playing shows, it means that they have

MAKING A FLYER

A flyer should be half about you, and half about what you are looking for. Before you make the flyer, figure out some specifics. Would you rather it be all-girls? Do you want to play a specific style of music? Do you want to play shows, or just play for fun on weekends? How should people contact you? You don't have to get too deep, but explain enough to attract people with similar interests. Specify or imply how old you are, and that you are looking to be in bands with people around your own age, so you don't get calls from thirty-five-year-old guys asking you to join their reggae cover band.

The flyer doesn't need to give the perfect description of your band or list all of your influences. You just have to put out the basic idea: "Hard-hitting drummer wanted for metal side project" is enough. It's tempting to list all the bands you've ever listened to, but this flyer is just an ad and it should be short and to the point. Here are some examples.

BASS AND KEYS LOOKING FOR GUITARIST AND SINGER FOR ROCK BAND

Bass player and keyboardist, 15 & 14, are looking for guitarist and female singer for rock band.

Influences: Arcade Fire, early Doors, and Rihanna. Must be able to practice after school, on weekends, and play shows.

Contact:
xxxxxxx@gmail.com

LOOKING FOR DRUMMER FOR ALL-GIRL JAM BAND

We are looking for a girl drummer, age 13–15, to join our sixteen-piece jam band. Must be able to sing, play quietly, and have own drums. Chimes a plus. We play dreamy, spacey pop. Must be into Radiohead and Phish. No drugs. Myspace.com/ xxxxxxx

SINGER LOOKING TO START BAND

Looking for other serious beginner musicians to play with once a week and work on songs

I am into everything but country and rap-metal. My songs are a cross between Panic at the Disco, mid-'80s Poco and Linkin Park.

CALL XXX-XXX-XXXX

KEYS TO KEEPING YOUR BAND TOGETHER

1. Be patient with yourself and the rest of your band. When one person stresses, the whole band stresses.

2. Be the band's leader, not the band's boss.

3. Fight for your ideas when they're really important to you, but don't dominate the whole band. Choose your battles. Always insisting on doing it your way isn't fair.

4. Encourage and support each other; be a team. It's cheesy but true: just like there is no "I" in team, there is no "I" in band either.

5. Be reliable. The more you trust each other, the better your band will be. Stick to the practice schedule, don't flake, and show up prepared.

songs and are established in some way. Joining their band means learning to play what they have written and maybe not contributing or writing music with them. The term "original," when used in a flyer, doesn't mean unique. It means that the band writes its own songs. Many musicians are perfectly happy playing their favorite songs instead of creating their own—a band that only plays other people's songs is called a cover band. A cover band is different from a tribute band. A tribute band tries to sound exactly like a certain band, and may also dress up like them; it's the Halloween of band styles.

LET'S STAY TOGETHER: KEEPING THE PEACE IN YOUR BAND

In every band there are cliques, allegiances, and little rivalries—such as the rhythm section that always pairs together, the guitarists who are always trying to outdo each other. This is natural. Be careful not to let those divisions or partnerships interfere with band unity. After a bad practice, it's easy to hang out with your best bandmate, complain about the bassist, and blame them for the fact that your new song doesn't feel right. While this might seem harmless because you aren't saying it to her face, it only serves to make things worse by instilling a sense of "us versus them." You are all on the boat together. If you start kicking holes in the floor, everyone is going to sink.

ENDLESS, NAMELESS: FINDING A NAME

Back in the day, performers used names that explained what they were about. There was no MySpace page to check out; there were only records sold in a little bin in the back of the

EVERYDAY I WRITE THE BOOK

Whether you are starting a band later today or sometime next summer, begin keeping a list of potential band names. Take a dollar down to the drugstore and buy a pocket-size notebook, and when you think of a name, or spot a cool word in a book, write it down. Whatever you don't use as a band name might make for a good song or album title.

dime store, so you had to have a name that enticed people.

Blues musicians often put a descriptive word or nickname in front of their names (Mississippi John Hurt, Big Mama Thornton, or Blind Willie McTell). Names that distinguish where a band is from (Cincinnati Jug Band, the Chicago Women's Liberation Rock Band, New York Dolls, for instance), can be helpful because some cities are known for certain styles of music. A big city implies a kind of cosmopolitan flash; using the name of a dusty town in the South can suggest that the music is authentic or simple. If you play the kind of music that your city or region is known for, communicating that can be useful, but it can also be cliché. Sometimes, performers use a word to sell you on their talent (The Supremes, The Notorious B.I.G., The Fabulous Thunderbirds). Punk and metal bands often have tough or violent-sounding names as an extension of their message or sound (Crass, Bikini Kill, Poison Idea, Slayer).

You can pick a band name that reflects your sound, your ideas, or the lineup of your band. You can come up with a name that reflects your political discontent (The Clash, Anti-Flag, Rage Against the Machine). If you are a female Rolling Stones tribute band, you can use a famous Stones song title as a band name (Honky Tonk Women, Mother's Little Helpers) to let people know what you're about.

Coming up with a decent, memorable band name is hard. Usually, all the good names you've thought up are taken, no one in the band can agree, and the bassist is insisting on something atrocious like Vomitstorm. Choosing a name can take weeks or even months, with every band practice ending in fifteen minutes of brainstorming and picking names out of someone's shoe. (This is why I always try to join bands with names already.) The good news is that once you come up with a name and stick with it, you are done and you never, ever have to do it again. The accepted rule is that once you've played your first show, stick with the name you have.

Bikini Kill's girl power message inspired many women to start their own bands.

16 WAY OVERUSED WORDS IN BAND NAMES

- ★ Super
- ★ Wolf
- ★ Star
- ★ Fire
- ★ Bird
- ★ Crystal
- ★ Blood
- ★ Earth
- ★ Boy
- ★ Girl
- ★ Love
- ★ Party
- ★ Black
- ★ White
- ★ Blue
- ★ Rainbow

Depending on your audience, your name is going to have different connotations, so there's no sense trying to find the one flawless band name that perfectly evokes what your band is about. As long as the name isn't easily confused with another band's (Pearl Yam, The Be-Dulls), more than four words long, or totally offensive, whatever you end up with will be just fine. Pick one, make sure it's yours and yours alone, and roll with it.

In the past twenty or thirty years, it's become common to have a band name that doesn't mean much (Pavement, Xasthur, CAN, No Age)—and doesn't give you a clue what the band sounds like. You can call your piano-driven power-pop duo the Hot Garbage Polka Revue, Bobby Jr., or Hair Pollution, and the difference between your sound and what the name implies gives the name its meaning. You don't have to be exact and call yourselves the Tender Piano-Tinkling Two.

MAKE SURE THAT NAME IS YOURS TO USE

When you find a band name you like, before you get too attached to it, thoroughly search the Internet to make sure another band doesn't already have that same name. If you're going to make recordings or play anywhere outside of your basement, you *must* have an original name; otherwise, people might confuse your band with another band, which can lead to trouble. You don't want to be playing shows and making records for a few years and suddenly get a letter from a lawyer informing you that a horrible hippie band from New Jersey that hasn't put out a record since 1973 legally owns your name. Once you have checked on the Internet (try a couple of places—Google, iTunes, Ultimate Band List, and MySpace), you can double-check by calling a record store and asking if there are bands with similar names.

When you are done doing that, you can triple-check by going to the U.S. Trademark database and searching that your name doesn't overlap with anyone's trademark. A trademark is a legal way to protect your band's name as well as any images that identify your band so others can't use them.

1 Start at www.uspto.gov

2 Then go to the "Trademarks" link on the left-hand side and click on "Search TM database."

3 Then click on: New User Form Search (Basic) and type in your proposed band name.

TRADEMARKING YOUR BAND NAME

If a band decides to sue another band with the same name, the law favors whoever was using the name first. You may have been The JoJo Dancers for four years already, but maybe The JoJo Dancer Band in Richmond trademarked the name last month. Because they put the effort into trademarking the name, they can legally get you to change the name.

Trademarks are also the reason you can't name your band Burger King or Coca-Cola; if a brand or product is popular enough, they can sue you by charging that you are profiting off their popularity. Which means that you can't name your band The Coca-Cola Kid either. The other basis for a band name lawsuit has to do with confusion. Let's say that you call your band Cadillac Treehouse—it's a band and not likely to be confused with a car—so you are probably okay, but not all corporations are going to be cool with your use of their brand name. If your band's name is close to another band's name—especially if you have the same or similar sounding words, you will get a cease-and-desist letter from that band's lawyer sooner than you think.

If you do start to get really serious about your band—especially if you are about to sign a record deal, and/or are

HIT THE BOOKS:

A LESSON IN HERSTORY

Here are a few books to educate you about great female performers who have come before.

She's a Rebel: The History of Women in Rock and Roll by Gillian G. Gaar (Seal Press, 2002). A wonderful book on female performers spanning the entire history of rocking 'n' rolling. Lots of inspiration and sass. This is the essential book to start with.

Swing Shift: All-Girl Bands of the 1940s by Sherrie Tucker (Duke University Press, 2000). Major history of women's contributions to the swing era.

Stormy Weather: The Music and Lives of a Century of Jazz Women by Linda Dahl (Limelight Editions, 1989). A history of women's overlooked involvement in jazz and blues, with a lot of information on Billie Holiday.

The Rolling Stone Book of Women in Rock: Trouble Girls by Barbara O'Dair (Random House, 1997). Behold a book of fifty-six essays by forty-four writers on artists from all eras and genres.

Girls Rock!: Fifty Years of Women Making Music by Mina Carson, Tina M. Lewis, and Susan M. Shaw (University of Kentucky Press, 2004). Biographies of a broad spectrum of female performers.

Cinderella's Big Score: Women of the Punk and Indie Underground by Maria Raha (Seal Press, 2004). Interviews and artist histories of women of the underground indie and punk music scenes, including Crass, Sleater-Kinney, Le Tigre, The Gossip, and riot grrrl.

making a living from playing music— you should register a trademark for your name. There are trademark services that do extensive searches of federal and state copyrights and trademarks that will tell you about any possible conflicting names.

Trademark services will also register your band's name, so that you are legally free and clear to keep playing as Clown Birthday, and won't have to become Clown Birthday UK if someone challenges you for the name. These services usually cost between $400 and $1,000 which, even though it's expensive, is way cheaper than fighting a lawsuit a few years down the line. Again, this isn't really necessary unless you are signing deals and your band is a full- or part-time career for you.

You can also get into trouble using the full names of living people, especially if they are famous. They can allege that you are trying to benefit from their fame. So, as tempting as it is, don't name your band Lindsay Lohan, Lindsay Lohan's Limo or The Lindsay Lohan Lost Weekend Trio. Fortunately, because of your first amendment rights, you can still use those as album or song titles. In America, you can say pretty much whatever you want in a song—you can sing about hating the president (à la Pink or Bright Eyes) or that you'd like to blow up Disneyland (Dils' "Blow Up Disneyland"), and that right is protected as an American and as an artist.

> "I demand perfection in what I do and I practice very hard before I give a concert—sometimes three to six hours a day. And I am particular about the seating of the audience—also about how much money they pay—but most of all where they are seated. If I am going to sing something intimate, who am I going to sing it to?"
>
> **NINA SIMONE**

(A lot of European countries, plus Canada, Singapore, Australia, and Brazil have much stricter laws that regulate speech, FYI.)

You can name your band after people who are long dead or are forgotten footnotes of ancient history; sitcom actors of the '70s, signers of the Declaration of Independence, Belgian tennis stars, or women's rights pioneers, for example.

SOURCES FOR BAND NAMES

Many a great band name has been born from cracking open a book and randomly pointing to a word on a page. Sometimes you need to pull from additional sources or find some other words to string together if your own vocabulary feels exhausted. Here are a few reliable sources to try.

★ Dictionaries of all kinds: foreign language dictionaries, slang dictionaries, a thesaurus

★ Online lists of portmanteau words (blended words—like spork, Reaganomics, Labradoodle)

★ History books

★ Collections of poetry

★ Wildlife encyclopedias

★ Maps

★ Other bands' lyrics

SOLITARY GIRL: BEING A SOLO ARTIST

Being a solo performer is just as fun as being in a band, and in most ways, it's easier. There is a lot more freedom. You don't have bandmates rearranging your ideas or sanding them down, so your songs are a pure expression of your creativity and exactly as you envision them. There's less equipment to lug around, and you never have to deal with people being late to practice.

Most solo acts are one person singing while playing an instrument—usually a guitar, but sometimes harp, drums, piano, accordion, banjo, computer, or cello. Your one-woman band can be anything you want: You can play music on your laptop. You can do an animal dance while you play timbales. You can perform bluegrass fiddle numbers with a tambourine attached to your foot to keep time. You can play a warped cassette through a boom box while screaming songs from *High School Musical*. You can strum an acoustic guitar and sing about how your broken heart is like a dead flower. You get the picture: You can be as traditional or as high-concept

32 FEMALE SOLO ARTISTS WHOSE LIVE PERFORMANCES YOU NEED TO CHECK OUT ON YOUTUBE

- ★ Cat Power
- ★ Taylor Swift
- ★ Feist
- ★ Sheila E
- ★ Etta James
- ★ Kate Bush
- ★ Erykah Badu
- ★ Mary Timony
- ★ Sinéad O'Connor
- ★ Frida Hyvonen
- ★ Patti Smith
- ★ Neneh Cherry
- ★ PJ Harvey
- ★ Carole King
- ★ Liz Phair
- ★ Yoko Ono
- ★ Diamanda Galas
- ★ Grace Jones
- ★ Carla Bozulich
- ★ Wynne Greenwood (a.k.a. Tracy and the Plastics)
- ★ Odetta
- ★ Björk
- ★ Dolly Parton
- ★ Roxanne Shante
- ★ Ani DiFranco
- ★ Sister Rosetta Tharpe
- ★ Cyndi Lauper
- ★ Loretta Lynn
- ★ Nina Hagen
- ★ Nina Simone
- ★ Janis Joplin
- ★ Joanna Newsom

as you feel inclined to be because you're in charge.

Being solo is the biggest vulnerability, but it can also be your biggest strength. One of the great gifts of a solo act is that there is much less of a barrier (that "I-am-the-performer-and-you-are-the-audience" mentality) between you and the audience. It's easier to have a personal connection when you are being real and bare, and there isn't the volume and action of a full band to hook people with. People get that being solo is a brave act. It doesn't always mean they are going to be more polite, but most people will be more respectful of a solo act than a band. People sometimes assume that solo performers are solo because they want all the attention on them. But by having a clear motivation and vision, by making some honest music—you will instantly change the audience's mind.

The other rad thing about being solo is that, when you're performing and the audience applauds, it's all for you. With that applause, you get to be fully aware of just how much the seven people gathered in your basement liked that Lil' Wayne cover you just did. The challenge is to be steadfast and not freak out if the audience isn't spellbound by your songs, or if they laughed during the sad one about when your hamster ate its babies. It's only natural to want people to be falling at your feet, requesting autographs and treating you like a rock goddess. But! But! But! If that doesn't happen (it might not), if most of the audience leaves during your set, if people heckle or boo you (jerks!), ignore it and go on to the next song.

A big part of performing is learning how to deal with an audience's reaction. You have to learn how to put your heart and mind into what you are doing even when the audience doesn't care. "They didn't like my songs" does not mean, "They didn't like me." You don't need to change your art to something that they can understand—just doing what you are doing over and over again will make them

> "The only thing you have to learn to be a rock singer is to just sound like yourself."
>
> **CHRISSIE HYNDE, THE PRETENDERS**

understand. Do your thing, whatever it is, and don't worry about tweaking it to please people who didn't get it. The people who appreciate what you are doing will stick around, and the ones that don't, fortunately, will get lost.

EXPRESS YOURSELF: LYRICS AND SONGWRITING

Until 1963, when Bob Dylan changed the game with his second album, rock lyrics were very literal and clichéd. Lots of easy rhymes about love, cars, dancing, and parties. Dylan came to rock from the folk music movement, which was heavily influenced by poetry and political songwriters like Woody Guthrie (he wrote "This Land Is Your

"Music is the beat of life for me. It's like my heart. You have to keep on going. Motivation is too light a word for it. It is life itself to me. It's like I have to keep on breathing, it's a way of survival, a way of being alive."

YOKO ONO

Land"). Dylan's lyrics were different from anything that came before. They were abstract, used complex metaphors, slang, snippets of conversation—and though he was singing about heartbreak, his friends, or politics, the words held a different meaning for everyone who heard them, not just a single, straightforward meaning that anyone would understand. Dylan was so influential, and this idea was so freeing, that many popular artists started to write songs that were real and honest, without happy endings, with metaphor, singing in a way that sounded like how people actually spoke to one another.

Whether your song is about an actual tree or a metaphorical tree depends on what kinds of songs you want to write. There aren't any rules to writing lyrics besides "be yourself." How your lyrics come out has to do with what inspires you and what you want to tell the world. This section will help you find your inspiration and start writing lyrics that express your ideas.

Your favorite singers might be what's inspiring you to start a band, so it's natural if the first songs you write are imitations of theirs. A personal writing style is something that you develop over time as you heap your own ideas in with your influences. The more you write and play, the more your own style will come out, and you'll move out from the shadow of your influences. Eventually getting out of that shadow is important because if you base your lyrics on someone else's, you'll wind up with a bunch of clichés instead of lyrics that are one hundred percent, authentically YOU.

WRITING IT DOWN

Whether you've got volumes of songs in your head or one vague idea, you're going to start the same way: by getting the words out of your head and onto paper. The first step is simple and it'll run you about three bucks: Buy two notebooks, one regular size and the other pocket size. Don't skimp by getting one medium size; you'll need both. The big notebook is for writing and editing lyrics and compiling your ideas. The little one is for when you are walking to the bus or at your friend's house and you're struck with a flash of brilliance, so you can get it down while it's fresh. The rule with the little notebook is this: KEEP IT WITH YOU AT ALL TIMES. Even if you're going on a date or spelunking in a dark cave, it should be in your pocket or bag. The one time you don't

have it is when you'll come up with THE BEST IDEA and no one within a quarter-mile radius will have paper or a pen and you'll be forced to write it in mint lip balm on a crinkled-up napkin. Don't trust that you'll be able to remember it, don't write it on your hand, and don't keep it in your BlackBerry. Writing ideas down in the little notebook isn't just about keeping track of them, it's about developing a skill that is essential to being a songwriter: thinking about your music all the time. You have to be in touch with your creative mind and nurture it *constantly*, and not just when there is a guitar on your lap.

Once you've handled the notebook situation, it's time to fill the pages. Start observing what happens around you and take notes. When people are speaking, listen for interesting words,

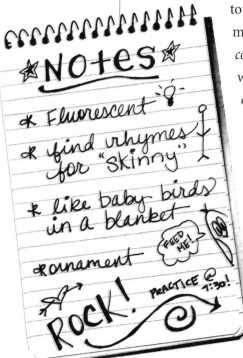

phrases, slang, slogans, and punch lines. Write down little details you notice—how things smell, look, how your sister acts when she's nervous. Paying attention to how people speak—how their voices rise and fall, the cadence and rhythms in conversation, the natural melodies of speech all can help you learn how to fit words into a song. The more you write down now, the more you'll have to pick and choose from later when you are working on songs. So, write and write and then write a little bit more, and do it every day. Pretty soon, it'll become second nature to do it and you'll reach for your notebook as soon as an idea starts to bloom in your mind.

THE WRITING PROCESS

Lyrics are a three-step process: inspiration, *then* writing, and *then* revisions. Inspiration is a matter of keeping your eyes and ears open to the world, and paying attention to your own mind and heart. Writing is simply putting that inspiration into words. Once you begin writing, you may need to keep reminding yourself that that's all

> "I had a guitar and I couldn't play, and I'd just write lyrics write lyrics write lyrics write lyrics write lyrics write lyrics."
>
> **COURTNEY LOVE**

you're doing: Just writing. Not writing *and* editing. Not writing *and* worrying whether your lyrics don't rhyme, that they might be lame, or that you've used "ocean" fourteen times. Giving yourself a hard time is not useful in the first stage of the creative process, and thus it is forbidden! You've got all the time in the world to edit and/or drive yourself crazy over the details; attempting to get it perfect on the first try (or second or third, for that matter) will only trip you up. Self-doubt is something all artists struggle with, but being self-critical *while* you are writing may stunt your growth as a lyricist, and you want to be full-size.

This is all you need to do: Put the words down as they come to you; let them spill out in a jumbled mess. Let the words and ideas flow out freely—don't stop them up with perfectionism. Even if what's coming out is a Niagara Falls of flowery stuff that you would never in a zillion years sing aloud—it doesn't matter. You are the only person who's going to see this. You can (and will) make sense of the words later. Let the words hang out on the page for at least a day or two before you start crossing things out and going wild with the eraser. Getting a little distance from them will help you come back fresh and you'll be able to tell the difference between a usable idea and sentimental barf.

When you come back to your notebook with a clear head, page through your little notebook and look for bright spots. When you spot words you like or feel moved by, copy them into the big notebook. Look for themes you can weave together and ideas that you want to expand upon. Play around with it, add to it, stare intently at it for a few minutes. When you are reading over what you've written, what jumps out at you? You might not know exactly what kind

MARY HAD A LITTLE SONG

One of the best ways to learn how to put words to music is to practice writing new lyrics to a song you already know. It can be "Mary Had a Little Lamb" or something by your favorite band—it doesn't matter so long as you are familiar with the tune and don't mind listening to it or humming it a bunch of times. This way you can get started even if you don't have a band or are starting with your instrument and not quite to the songwriting stage yet. By turning The Beatles' "Yesterday" into a song about how your sister's obsession with the Jonas Brothers refuses to die, you'll discover:

1. What it takes to fill a three-minute song.

2. How to write the verse, chorus, and verse structure.

3. Your own songwriting process.

> "I like being tough on stage. I don't like being sweet. I can't sing about love in the afternoon among the flowers and the sunshine. I like to sing about things that make me mad."
>
> **PAT BENATAR**

of song you're cobbling together until you start digging into it. Listen to your intuition and wander around some, and keep trying out different ideas until you find the ones that work.

When you begin fitting lines together, they will probably be a little wobbly. Like newborn-pony wobbly—you know, kind of cute and funny but topples over as soon as it tries to go anywhere. Be patient with the wobbly pony in your writing. Yelling at the pony does not help it learn how to trot any faster. This is just how baby ponies do it, they nosedive into a hay bale a couple of times until they understand how their knees work. You might have to stare at

the page and wobble for a while. You may have to try eleven or a hundred rhymes before you find the right one. Even if it feels fruitless, the stuff that doesn't work out is still teaching you. What isn't right for this song might be perfect for the one you write next month. Get the little ideas down and expand them into bigger ideas, turn the two words that sound cool together into a phrase, and then flesh that phrase into a section of the song. Do that again and again and again and eventually, you will wind up with a song.

WRITING WHAT YOU KNOW

Whether you think so or not, you already have plenty of life experience to base your songs on. Even if the life you lead feels unworthy of song, your friends/ city/school are totally boring, and the most exciting thing you've ever done was fall out of a tree house when you were seven, right there, in all that restlessness, injury, and boredom, you've got at least three songs—maybe even an album if you are especially clever about it. By developing your writing and observing skills, you can turn anything into a song.

Yes, anything. The Flaming Lips' singer Wayne Coyne wrote a pop song about a spider bite (appropriately titled "The Spider Bite Song"). Joanna Newsom wrote a song about not being able to write a song ("Inflammatory Writ"). Whether your songs are reactions to a war, are based on your fantasy life, or are telling a true story, there is really only one rule: *Write what you know.* Here are some questions to help you unearth what you know and chronicle it in song.

1 How are your feelings feeling? What's making you happy? Are you joyous and free? Anxious? Satisfied? Grateful? Are you a girl on the verge of an emo-meltdown?

2 You can't hide from love: Are you in love? Are you running from it? Toward it? Are you tortured by a crush on someone who isn't aware of your existence? True l-u-v is a many-splendored thing, but there's nothing like a painful breakup to help you summon up a few dozen songs. I'm not suggesting that you dump someone for the benefit of your art, but just remember that

blistering heartache is a powerful creative force if you harness it correctly. So if/when your heart is a mess, *milk it for all it's worth.* Chronicle the highest highs, those happy times when you had it all, the moment when that all changed, the sorrow, disgust, elation, and awful text messages that followed. Now, a note for those who haven't experienced romantic love: You can still write love songs. You don't have to lie, you just have to use your knowledge of other things you love (your pet/grandma/BFF). You can sing your heart out about how much you care, and unless you throw in lines about their shiny fur or start crooning "Ooh, Mittens, you're mine till the end of time"—no one will know the difference. It's not about the object of your affections; it's about the feeling.

3 What do you want? Total freedom? Better parties to go to? World peace? For every girl in the world to start a band? A black leather prom dress with your name airbrushed on it? Desire, like romantic pain, is easy to channel into songs—strong feelings usually are. What

HIT THE BOOKS:
THE WRITE STUFF

Here are two great books to get you primed for songwriting glory.

Songwriters on Songwriting, revised and expanded by Paul Zollo (Da Capo Press, 2003). 750 pages of interviews with the world's best songwriters of the last fifty years explaining how they compose, where their inspiration comes from, and all their songwriting secrets. Even if you don't care about Carole King or people who wrote songs for The Supremes, the interviews are fascinating and super useful for any songwriter.

Classic Rock Stories: The Stories Behind the Greatest Songs of All Time by Tim Morse (St. Martin's Griffin, 1998). Paul McCartney, Alice Cooper, Rod Stewart, and others spill the beans on classic jams.

you want from the world and what kind of life you want to lead aren't too big to tackle in a song.

4 What don't you want? Resistance is a strong feeling—it's desire in reverse. You can be serious and heavy and write about things close to your heart: your parents' divorce, sexism or other forms of injustice, how sad you feel when you see stray dogs eating trash. Pen an ode to your hatred of both mimes and pork chops—yes, in the same song! Channeling your anger, aggression, frustration, revenge fantasies, and loathing into song is really gratifying. (Just wait until you get to perform it!)

5 What have you read/seen/heard lately? Is there a story in the news that you're obsessing on? Did you read a book and wish you had the protagonist's jet-set life? Did you watch *The Sound of Music* and now have the urge to turn your bedroom curtains into a dress? It's possible to write about what you learned from a movie, a book, or the news without it sounding like that report you did on a Conestoga wagon train in third grade—you just have to make it personal. You can write about how it inspired you to change your life, or just your reaction to seeing it.

6 Something I learned today. High school is an evergreen topic for rock songs. Loving it and hating it, the friends and the feuds—all you have to do is come up with creative rhymes for "graduate" and you are halfway there. (P.S. The best time to write songs about high school is while you are still in it, since writing songs about how high school was the best time of your life is a cliché best left for cheesy classic-rock ballads.)

7 That's life. Write about your memories, what you do every day, where you hang out, where you go to get away, family, neighbors, your old house, your first friend, strangers you see around. Take it all apart, and then put it back together in a song. The Beach Boys' "In My Room" is a perfect example of turning a seemingly mundane,

everyday-life subject (being alone in your bedroom) into something special.

8 The song that won't exist until you write it. I started writing about music because everything I read about my favorite band was sexist and totally missed the point. I wanted someone who appreciated them like I did to put my feelings and fandom into words, but that seemed unlikely, so I had to do it myself. You are the only person who can write that song about your life, about some specific experience you had that you wish there was a song about. The responsibility is on you to fill that void.

> "My whole purpose with this thing is to communicate. What I sing is my own reality. But just the fact that people come up to me and say 'Hey, that's my reality, too' proves to me that it's not just mine."
>
> **JANIS JOPLIN**

Just so we're clear: Writing what you know doesn't mean that your lyrics have to be strictly autobiographical. There is no song law that says you have to put it all down exactly as it happened in real life. After all, Johnny Cash never actually shot a man in Reno just to watch him die. This is why being a songwriter is a more exhilarating prospect than being a court reporter. You only have to put down *your* truth, as it exists for you. You can embellish it, make it fantastic, and leave out the boring parts (you should). Dig deep into your imagination and subconscious and get as weird as you want. The only thing you need to consider is what *you* want to say. As the box below explains, you can apply your life experience to other stories.

ROCKING A MILE IN SOMEONE ELSE'S SHOES

You *can* write a song about a situation that you haven't actually gone through, like seeing a ghost or being a samurai trapped in a Dutch prison, if you weave your own knowledge of fear or sadness into the experience. Writing about a parallel situation can even be easier than writing about your own life, especially if you are writing about something that's personal and private or you don't feel comfortable making a song that is all "I, I, I, me, me, me." You can project your situation into someone else's life, another time, or another place. Instead of writing a very direct song about how you and your best friend are no longer best anything, you can turn you and her into brothers who work as security screeners at the Pittsburgh airport, and one of them is jealous of the other because he gets to run the X-ray machine all the time. Or you could write a song from her perspective, apologizing to you. It's just a matter of digging into the guts of the situation and feeling around for something to hold on to, making it real for you.

WORD UP

Writing what you know doesn't apply just to song topics and experiences. Some basic guidelines:

1. Don't use a word that you don't know the definition of.

2. Don't use words that you wouldn't use in regular conversation.

3. Complex words are fine as long as they are appropriate to the song.

4. Don't use words just to sound super-smart.

5. Don't use words just for the sake of rhyming.

Comparing your breakup to the cycle of cell meiosis would be a clunker in the middle of your average love song, but it'd work perfectly if the whole song uses chromosomes as a metaphor for romance. It's a fine line—an unusual or four-syllable word, if well placed, can help make your music really distinctive and original (Joanna Newsom and Fiona Apple are good examples of how to pull this off).

Recently, I saw an all-star band play their first show. It was packed, wall-to-wall, sold out—people wanted to see if the new band lived up to the hype. A few songs in, right in the middle of a perfectly enjoyable verse, the singer howled the word "STAAAAGECOOOOACH." It came out of nowhere, had nothing to do with the rest of the song, and everything to do with his wanting us to think he's weird/cool. His eyes were shut so he missed what really happened, which was the whole audience trading looks of embarrassment. Showing off to the audience that you are especially smart or cool is neither smart nor cool. While you shouldn't be *overly* concerned with pleasing your audience, your words should be in service of the song. Going all "stagecoach" on them will rudely awaken the audience from their dreams of your song.

This may sound like a total no-brainer, but stick to writing lyrics in the language(s) you speak. If you can speak another language, by all means, sing in it or mix it in with English or whatever else you are fluent in. But if you don't speak French/Spanish/Yiddish, etc., I don't recommend writing a song in that language—it'll wind up being funny for all the wrong reasons. (This goes for attempting a foreign accent, too—unless you have an excellent excuse, like you are fronting a U2 cover band for Halloween and are going as a leprechaun instead of as Bono.)

Learn from this real-life example: David Lee Roth, the raspy, big-haired guy who once sang for Van Halen, famously put out a Spanish-language version of his record *Eat 'Em and Smile* entitled *Sonrisa Salvage*, despite the fact that he didn't actually know Spanish. The album came out in 1986, and even though the record company immediately canned it, people are still laughing about it today.

> "When I was younger, I didn't have that many chances to experience women playing rock music. Most of the women I've admired had to reinvent the genre for themselves."
>
> **KAREN O, YEAH YEAH YEAHS**

Lastly, a word of warning that will probably make you think I'm ninety-eight years old and typing this with my cane: Don't swear in a song unless you truly feel you need to. Swearing *can* create powerful emphasis, so save it up until you really need it (The Pretenders' "Precious" is a good example of how far just one word can go). But swearing a lot will make you sound inarticulate, crass, and/or stupid. I say this to you as a woman whose record collection is a veritable menagerie of every foul word you can imagine, who swears and appreciates the artistic and social merits of cussing from time to time. I'm also someone who, when I was younger, added generous helpings of the f-word into my conversations and songs because I thought this was the "punk" thing to do. I thought it made me sound sophisticated and tough. Instead, it made me sound like a kid who was trying waaaay too hard, which is exactly what I was. Bottom line: You're a songwriter, not a curmudgeonly old sea captain, so don't sell your rage short with random cursing.

EDITING YOURSELF

Maybe you gush *Order of the Phoenix*–length masterpieces the very second your pen touches the paper, but for most songwriters, lyric-writing is a process of compiling ideas and then editing them down. Editing is where you cross out, erase, and groom the words until they start to convey beauty, excitement, or your message to the aliens—whatever it is that you are trying to express in the song.

Editing yourself is, for some of us, about as much fun as reading the phone book. For me, it's not so much boring as it is embarrassing. When I start going over what I've written, I see all my lame word choices and ideas that seemed brilliant at the time and my ego deflates. Anyhow, a fortunate thing will happen to you as you go over your notebooks. You will hit patches of not-bad, some well-done phrases, and some parts where you'll marvel at your cleverness and go "Ooh, I did *that?*" and be a little impressed with yourself. Then you will realize that you are not a hideous failure. Or even a part-time sorta failure. You, in fact, are onto something—a good song will come out of these weird little pieces. So you just have to be brave and dive in and start cleaning and shaping it up.

Editing your lyrics is some of the hardest work you'll do, so resist the temptation to be too harsh a critic of your own work. What you are doing when you edit is ferreting out the good from the just-okay stuff, and then polishing those good parts until they gleam and the song becomes the golden nugget you want it to be. This may involve rearranging only a couple of words. It could also mean that you scrap everything but one flawless line. When you are editing, all you need to be asking yourself is "What do I really want to say here?" or "What am I trying to communicate?" or "How do I connect this verse to this chorus?" Those three things are enough to steer by. Do not ask yourself "Why do I suck?" or wonder if you might be in need of a brain transplant. Editing is a bit like brushing your hair: You have to work out the tangles gently, or else you are going to rip your hair out.

Songwriting is your art, and it's worth fussing over the details. Fuss all you want, but remember that having mean conversations with yourself in your head is not going to make you a better songwriter. It'll only make your creative brain scared and not want to come out of its cave and make art with you.

WHICH CAME FIRST: THE MUSIC OR THE LYRIC?

How you go about transforming your pages of rough scribbles into a proper song depends on whether you are writing the lyrics first or the music first. One has to be written to fit the other, and one way isn't better than the other—it simply depends on your method and that of your band. If you are the singer in your band and don't play an instrument, you are going to be at the mercy of your bandmates, so in the meantime, go ahead and work out your lyrics so that you can have some options to work from once the music is done.

SOMETIMES I RHYME SLOW, SOME TIMES I RHYME QUICK

Back in the day, around the twelfth to fourteenth centuries, people started writing songs that rhymed because it made them easier to remember, which was important, because back then songs might be hundreds or thousands of lines long, take days to perform, and would tell the entire story of a twenty-year-long war in great detail.

Rhyming makes a song easier to remember, but it also makes things sound tidy and clean around the edges. Because most songs do rhyme, and there are only so many words to rhyme together and still have a song make realistic sense, this has helped create a lot of clichés—think of the millions of songs that rhyme "baby" and "maybe."

Coming up with your own creative rhymes that communicate what you actually want to say can be a challenge, but it can be done. You may have to think on it for a few days to find what pairs up well with the phrase "tanning bed," for instance, but getting a rhyming dictionary is a big help. You can buy one

ANATOMY OF A SONG

Intro A part that comes at the start of a song, is often slow, almost always instrumental, before the song or first verse kicks in.

Verse The verse comes after the introduction but before the chorus.

Pre-chorus Comes just before the chorus; it ramps the song up to the chorus.

Chorus Repeats throughout the song, usually after each verse.

Bridge Transitional part that happens once between two parts in a song, usually introduces a new musical theme (it doesn't have a hook) and happens near the end of a song between the second and third chorus. Only some songs have them.

Solo A part where a single performer's part comes to the forefront. The rest of the band might drop out and you just hear that person go nuts for a little bit. Sometimes happens during the bridge.

Spoken Interlude Where the music drops out or gets quiet and someone speaks rather than sings.

Outro Final part of the song, usually instrumental, might repeat the hook of the chorus but without the singing.

(*Oxford Complete* is good) and there are also some rhyming sites online. In his book *Tunesmith*, the songwriter Jimmy Webb (he wrote "By the Time I Get to Phoenix"), suggests looking up the rhymes that go with the words that are your central theme or song title, and then making a list of the ones that make sense. Doing this before you start writing helps prevent you from painting yourself into a corner. If you're super-committed to having your songs rhyme, this is not a bad idea, so that you don't get halfway into your chorus and find that the only thing that rhymes with "kumquat" is "blood clot"—a word that's far too gross to put in your tropical-fruit anthem.

The downside of rhyming lyrics is that it constrains things; you're stuck

"I think when you see women in music people assume it's just a girl, and that's the gimmick, and there's some mastermind man behind the scenes doing all the actual work. That was really the only seriously big challenge for me, being a woman in the industry. I had to prove that I was real, and that I'm actually a writer first and a singer and performer second."

AMY LEE, EVANESCENCE

with "You and me / We're going to be free" despite that what you mean to say is "You and I / Are ditching class and going to the beach." Rhyming just for the sake of rhyming can get you into dangerous territory pretty quick, so consider your other options—which are: not rhyming, not rhyming all the time, and not being so strict with your end rhymes. For example, you can also tie things together by having a sound or vowel that repeats, as in Journey's 1981 megahit, the number one downloaded song of all time, "Don't Stop Believin'":

A singer in a smoky room
A smell of wine and cheap perfume

The way Steve Perry sings it, the "i" is emphasized in "singer" and sounds like "eeee." That vowel sound comes up again in "smoky" and "cheap"; the repeated "i" in "wine," and in the following line in "smile," and "night." The "room"/ "perfume" rhyme pulls everything together. Add to that the repetition of "on" in the next verse, which soars off into the stratosphere and leads us into a solo that mimics that repetition and creates a rhythm that keeps the song together. INTENSE!

Or you can rhyme every couple of lines. If you listen to "Don't Stop Believin'", focus on the song's next verse. The words "win" and "born," and then "dice" and "time" are *slant-rhymed*.

Slant rhymes, are when two words don't rhyme perfectly, but end with the same letter or sound. It's not as tidy, but depending on how you sing it, you can make words sound pretty close. Slant rhymes don't fence you in as much as when you are committed to exact matches in your rhyme scheme. The main thing is not to go off course in the song, just to make something fit the rhyme scheme; the *Oxford Dictionary of Rhymes* suggests "horseleech" as a rhyme for "beach," which you could tie together if your verse is about a disastrous trip to the river, but if that's not where you are going—don't go there.

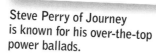

Steve Perry of Journey is known for his over-the-top power ballads.

DON'T BORE US, GET TO THE CHORUS

There is a saying "Don't bore us, get to the chorus"—which explains what a chorus is: the part of the song that you *really* want to hear. It's the meat in the sandwich of the song. The chorus is almost always where the "hook" is; the hook is the catchiest and most memorable part of the song—it grabs your attention and makes you want to sing along. It's where the basic message of the song is, and is usually the least complicated part of the song. It also answers the questions raised by the verses. The verses build up the tension, so the listener wonders what's going to happen next, and then, voilà! The chorus arrives and relieves that tension. (If "tension relief" reminds you more of a backrub than a song, think of it more like an "A-ha!—the tiny mystery is solved!" moment.) Say the verse is about how school is boring, and you just want to dance and forget your problems; the chorus would then be about how you are at the best party of your life and you are going to dance all night. For a real example, let's take a look at Hüsker Dü's "I Apologize."

Hayley Williams began singing in Paramore when she was fifteen.

Verse:

All these crazy mixed-up lies
Floating all around
Making these assumptions
brings me down
And you get tight-lipped, how do I know
what you think?
Is it something I said when I lost my mind?
Temper too quick, makes me blind

Chorus:

I apologize . . .
Said I'm sorry, now it's your turn
Can you look me in the eyes and apologize?

In the verse, Bob Mould sings about drama that's brewing. Then, in the chorus, he takes the blame (sort of). The chorus is the explanation or resolution of what's happened in the verse. A chorus can offer a solution, it can be a punch line to the joke, it can reveal the name of the crush you sung about in the verse. The main thing is that there is a relationship between these two parts of the song. There should be a progression—even if it's simply what would naturally occur next. If the first verse is where you meet someone special, then the chorus is where you take it the next level, as in the Ronettes' "Be My Baby," which was written by Phil Spector, Jeff Barry, and Ellie Greenwich.

Verse:

The night we met
I knew I needed you so
And if I ever had the chance
I'd never let you go
So won't you say you love me
I'll make you so proud of me
We'll make 'em turn their heads
Every place we go
So won't you please

Chorus:
Be my, be my baby
Be my little baby
My one and only baby
Say you'll be my darling
Be my, be my baby
Be my baby now
My one and only baby.

She meets someone, she thinks this person's the one, so she pleads her case. Here she sings "baby" more than a dozen times in about two and a half minutes. Her message is clear. And what do you do with babies? You love and take extra special care of them—so she's implying she's going to be dedicated and adoring. "Be My Baby" uses a technique that a lot of choruses do in repeating a word over and over. It's the simplest way to get things across, to beat you over the head with a word, though that word might have multiple ideas behind it. In the early days of rock 'n' roll, that was pretty much how it went—that chorus was the title of the song repeated a few times in a row. A modern example of that is "Hello Hello" by Paramore, which repeats

words ("hello" and "now") *and* phrases ("sorry to hear").

A chorus shouldn't have more than two ideas (tops, and only if it's a special occasion). The chorus should be like a giant #1 fan foam finger pointing to your main idea. It doesn't have to be dumb, or super-obvious—just don't introduce some random new idea in there. If you listen to the chorus of The Rolling Stones' "Satisfaction," it has Mick Jagger summarizing everything he's said so far with two words— "no" and "satisfaction."

"I'm not the quickest, most prolific writer. I would never pretend to be. I don't think prolific-ness is equal to quality at all. I would rather have one song that people actually like than 15 songs that they can barely stand."

**KIM DEAL, THE PIXIES/
THE BREEDERS**

The chorus of The Clash's "London Calling" doesn't have repeating lines, and though there's a lot of action, there are only two ideas: environmental collapse/the apocalypse is coming this way, and singer Joe Strummer isn't afraid of it.

> *The ice age is coming,*
> *   the sun is zooming in*
> *Engines stop running and*
> *   the wheat is growing thin*
> *A nuclear error,*
> *   but I have no fear*
> *London is drowning—and I*
> *   live by the river.*

VERSES, OR HOW DO YOU GET TO FREE RIDE?

The job of the verse is to fill in the details of the song's message or story. Verses are more frilly and complex; they are the bread-crumb trail that leads us to the chorus. Let's examine the classic rock song "Free Ride" by the Edgar Winter Group. The chorus, when removed from the rest of the song, is rather vague.

> *Come on and take a free ride (free ride!)*
> *Come on and sit here by my side*
> *Come on and take a free ride.*

"What I look for in a song is for the story to be for real. I like a blood and guts kind of thing. That's what you find in the lyrics of country music. I do not want to be categorized and I don't want a label put on me. I won't stay in a little box; I want to sing what I want to sing."

ETTA JAMES

At this point, the song could be about hopping on the PeopleMover at Epcot Center for all we know. The verses explain:

First verse:
> *The mountain is high*
> *The valley is low*
> *And you're confused on which way to go*
> *So I've come here to give you a hand*
> *And lead you into the promised land*
> *So . . .*

Second verse:

> All over the country I've seen it the same
> Nobody's winning at this kind of game
> We've got to do better, it's time to begin
> You know all the answers must come from
>   within
> So . . .

So . . . the verse leads us to understand that "Free Ride" isn't about Edgar's Six Flags birthday, but rather, that glorious ride we call life.

The Fiery Furnaces' song "Benton Harbor Blues" has a simple chorus, sung by a sad-sounding Eleanor Freidberger:

> As I try to fill all of my empty days
> I stumble round on through my
>   memory's maze
> Of all my past, only the sadness
>   stays.

The chorus doesn't ask any questions, but the three verses that follow give us the answers:

> I was moping down by the bridge
> I rode a bike in the snow to the
>   mini-mart
> I thought of the ways that I've broke
>   my own heart

> It's not for me to fill the blue sea with tears
> But when I think back on all the wasted
>   years
> All the good cheer and all of the charm
>   disappears

> I wore the exact same clothes for five days
> The bail bondsman gave me a smile
> I was just thinking of only my sins all the
>   while.

How are those days getting filled? She's hitting the mini-mart and maybe doing a little jail time. What's she remembering?

Eleanor Freidberger started the Fiery Furnaces with her brother in 2000.

Bad things she's done to herself and other people. Why is she still sad? Because she can't forget the life she's led.

The typical rock song has two or three verses. This isn't a rule; it's just how most people do it. Unless you sing in a band that has superfast, nine-minute-long songs (e.g., Mars Volta), you have a limited amount of time to do your explaining. Writing a song isn't like writing a story—you are not obligated to tell us who, what, where, and why; there doesn't have to be a clear beginning or ending.

Now, there *is* a way to get across a good bit of information without putting the audience to sleep, and while it doesn't work all the time, it does work sometimes. Tell them a story. A story that goes in a straight line is best; something they can follow pretty easily. A suspenseful story with a surprise ending is a sure thing. Even if a story isn't that good, people want to know how it ends, and will stick it out so they aren't left wondering. That's just human nature. Here are two examples. Both are loooong classic rock songs that have been playing on the radio for more than thirty years. One is Gordon Lightfoot's "The Wreck of the Edmund Fitzgerald," which used to scare the living daylight out of me when I was little. At the beginning, a big ship and its crew sets out on Lake Superior; a half-dozen epic verses later, the ship's at the bottom and everyone is dead. Based on a true story, it's a morbid naval disaster made compelling.

The other example is one of the best-known rock songs of all time. You've heard it at least thirty-eight times without even trying. That's right: The Eagles' "Hotel California." Even though it's not my favorite song, it's impossible to turn it off when it comes on the radio. And the solo just can't be denied. In six

and a half minutes, Don Henley goes from high-living rich dude checking into a luxury hotel to realizing he's probably dead and is eating dinner in a fiery abyss. INTENSE! Through each verse, more weirdness is revealed, until we come to the "gotcha" ending:

> *"You can check out any time you like But you can never leave!"*

One of the things that "Hotel California" is a good example of is the idea that each verse builds dramatic intensity. The story should build and build, and the intensity will get popped by the final chorus, and the listener will feel triumph or relief. The drama doesn't have to be *drama*-drama, it needn't be the musical equivalent of a cafeteria fight posted on YouTube. It can be that something gets realized, or that you go from hopeless to hopeful, you started out in like and you wind up in love—or, if you're adventurous, downtown Pittsburgh. While your entire song might be about how swim camp is awesome, having three verses, two choruses, and an outro that *all* say that

"Rock 'n' roll is our cultural voice. I saw it evolve in my lifetime . . . and it was revolutionary, in every way. It gave young people an outlet."

PATTI SMITH

is going to be boring. The first verse could be about how you've been going to swim camp since you were six and you hated it at first, the second verse could be about your favorite memories, and the third verse will be about the friends you made and that you'll keep going till you're 102. The whole song is still about your love of camp, but it ramps up toward the end—we get a parting shot of your undying love. It's a bit of a *finale,* rather than a regular old *ending.*

The ramping-up doesn't have to be chronologically ordered. Another way to make a song dramatic is to start with a moment that would usually be the end, with the verses explaining what led up to that moment. Reversing the order can create suspense that you might not get from telling it in sequence.

THE RULES OF NO RULES

The funny thing about the rules of songwriting is that you don't have to follow them. At all. Especially if you don't feel like it. If there is a different song setup that serves your song best, go with it. A verse doesn't have to be followed by a chorus, a song doesn't have to start with a verse, you can have a song without a chorus. There are tons of books and websites that will tell you all songs *have* to go verse-chorus-verse-chorus-bridge-chorus, and, sure, that's how most bands structure their songs. There is no one right way that a song

"My real first time onstage was a talent show I did with my best friend Colleen in sixth grade, doing a tap dance to Buddy Holly's 'Every Day.' We practiced it about a million times and we were perfect, and that was my first real time of going, 'Okay, this is happening. This is what I'm going to do.'"

STEVIE NICKS, FLEETWOOD MAC

should go, and anyone who tells you otherwise is lying. Have one chorus and one verse. If your chorus is amazing, repeat it four times. Have a twenty-two-minute instrumental bridge between the second verse and the third chorus. Mess around with structure until you find what works for you.

The Radiohead song "Everything in Its Right Place" doesn't have a clear message ("Yesterday I woke up sucking a lemon" repeated four times?!), and the verses don't explain much of anything about the possibly nonexistent chorus. Still, the song is flawless. From what we can tell, it might be all verses. There are parts of the song that repeat and there are sounds that are emphasized, but ultimately, it's pretty free-form since there's no way to distinguish between verses and choruses. Radiohead rarely

Thom Yorke of Radiohead wrote his first song when he was eleven.

follows the standard rules of songwriting, which is part of the reason they are such a great band.

WHAT MAKES A GOOD SONG?

Writing a good song isn't like baking a cake. You can't check ingredients off a list and wind up with a particular product at the end.

Your mom, a rock critic, your drummer's brother—each has a different idea about what makes a song great. For them, maybe everything but the smoothest smooth jazz that ever smoothed makes them want to claw their face off.

There is only one barometer for whether a song is good: your heart. It's not just your heart, though—it's more of an ears/feelings combo. Do you have fun playing your song? Do you get excited to hear it? Does the song express

Practice can be the most fun part
of being in a band.

PRACTICE, PRACTICE, PRACTICE

Practice doesn't always make perfect, but it will give you two of the things you need the most, which are hard to get by any other means: confidence and knowing your way around your instrument. Perfection is overrated anyway—hitting all the right notes at the right time is great, but it's nothing without energy and inspiration to back it up. Which means you should practice, and practice a lot.

There are all sorts of things that count as practice. It can be teaching yourself scales out of a book, it can be playing along with lessons on YouTube or figuring out what sorts of weird noises you can get your guitar to make. Practicing is getting to know your instrument and how to use it.

Practicing with a band is altogether different from solo practice. Band practice is writing songs and learning songs, and then playing them a million

your ideas? That's all you really need to worry about. If you enjoy your music, and you put passion and energy into what you are doing, it will attract other people. The people who like your kind of music will find *you*.

times until they're memorized and thoroughly etched into your brain. When you have a show coming up or are about to make a recording, you want to get your songs to be as flawless as you can. And even if they are flawless in practice, at the show your drummer might be nervous and speed up, or you might forget the genius lyrics you came up with—but the more comfortable you are with the songs, the less likely those things are to happen. If the whole band is well-rehearsed, one person's mistake is much less noticeable and won't derail the whole song. Learning your songs inside and out can sometimes be a boring hassle, but once you have the satisfaction of walking offstage and knowing you *killed* it, you'll never question running through a song five times in a row again.

Unfortunately, finding a place where you can practice is not as easy as it is for adults, who can just go rent a practice space. For now, you're probably stuck talking your parents into letting you make amplified noise in the house on a regular basis. Perhaps they'll be delighted to host your practices in the living room, but chances are they'll want you some place farther away—attics, basements, and garages are the usual rehearsal spots.

Sound is like water—it'll leak out anyplace it can. Whatever practice spot is available, it's important to soundproof it to ensure that you're allowed to keep practicing there. Even if your band is the raddest thing this side of the New Jersey Turnpike, chances are the people next door do not want to hear your drum solo again. And again. And again.

It's hard to make a space truly soundproof, so the best thing to do is try to muffle and block the sound as much as possible. See the suggestions over the next few pages for "baffling" and other sound muffling techniques that can help you turn any room into a decent practice space.

HOW TO BAFFLE

These panels are easy to make, can be stored under your bed or in the back of a closet and are really handy regardless of where you practice or what instrument you play. These directions are for panels that fit inside windows, but there are multiple ways to use them.

WHAT YOU WILL NEED:

- ★ Measuring tape
- ★ Several large pieces of cardboard, or a couple of medium cardboard boxes (depending on the size and shape of your windows)
- ★ Pencil
- ★ Scissors or box cutter
- ★ Roll of duct or masking tape
- ★ Quilted moving blanket
- ★ 2 feet of twine or heavy string per panel (optional)
- ★ Hammer and nails (optional)

1 Measure the length and width of the inside of the window frame.

2 Mark and carefully cut two pieces of cardboard to those measurements. (If you don't already have large pieces of cardboard, you can tape some smaller pieces together.) Try to be exact—you want the cardboard to fit into the window frame as tightly as possible.

3 Lay one of the cardboard panels on the floor. Lay the moving blanket on top of it and fold and arrange the blanket until it fits on the panel—which means folding it in half or in thirds, depending on the size of the blanket. Securely tape the folded blanket in place.

blanket · tape · cardboard

4 Lay the second panel over the taped panel (so the blanket is sandwiched between the cardboard) and line up all the sides. Tape the sides of the panels together to seal them completely.

5 Press it into your window frame. Depending on what type of window you have, you may be able to make the panel sit snug on your windowsill. If not, you will have to gently tape it in.

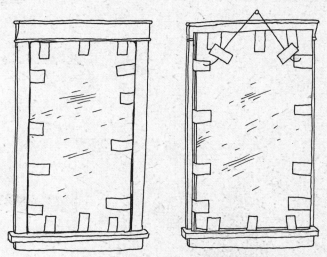

VARIATION:

If your panel doesn't fit in your window, you may choose to hang it. Use tape to attach a 2' length of twine toward the edge of your panel. Mark on the wall above the window where you'd like the panel to hang. Check with your parents before you start driving nails into your wall. With their permission/help, hammer one or two nails halfway into the wall above the window. Hang your panel and adjust as necessary.

SOUNDPROOFING

Baffle panels (previous page) are useful for more than blocking sound through the windows. You can prop them behind, around, or against a drum set, which can help muffle the banging. You can lean one against the door, instead of covering the door with a blanket. If you have a practice space that is just for your band (meaning it's not where someone sleeps or your dad parks the car), hang a panel at an angle above the drum kit. Aside from acting as insulation, these panels help direct the sound in a room. Sound bounces between parallel flat surfaces, which will make things sound clangy and bad. That is why in recording studios, every wall is at an angle. This stuff is not super important when you first start practicing, but it all makes a difference, and is good for you to know and understand.

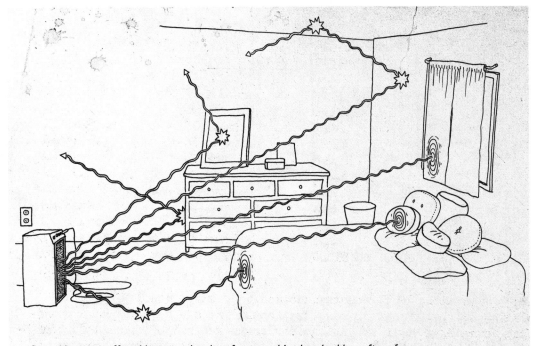

Sound bounces off and between hard surfaces, and is absorbed by soft surfaces.

5 WAYS TO KEEP IT DOWN WHEN YOU TURN IT UP

Rugs, leftover pieces of carpet or foam, pillows, towels, and blankets are all usable materials for muffling sound. Here are some ideas for quieting down a practice space.

1 Point amps away from windows, doors, and garage doors.

2 Prop your amp on a milk crate or a chair. Getting it off the floor keeps the vibrations from traveling through the floor.

3 Make a "baffle" (panel) to fit the windows. (See directions on pages 92 and 93.)

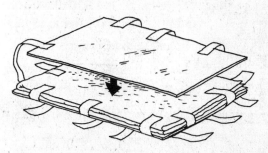

4 If you are practicing in a room (not a garage), take the end of a moving blanket (a cheap padded blanket, like a comforter but denser) and put it over the top of the door, and then shut the door to snug the blanket in place. The blanket should cover the length of the door.

5 Fold a bath towel in half and roll it up. It should be about the same width as the door. Snug the towel up against the inside bottom of the door. If you want, use a little bit of masking tape to secure it.

PRACTICING GUITAR ALONE IN YOUR ROOM

Sometimes, even when your volume knob is just barely above 2, somebody will complain. Practicing alone, on a little amp, you don't need to be very loud, but there is a way to turn it up and get away with it: You make a tent. See box, next page, for directions how.

MAKING DRUMS QUIETER

How do you make drums quieter? It's one of the world's great questions. Music stores sell pads and rubber mats that will mute the sound of your drums to a quiet thunk, but there is a cheap and easy solution in a drawer near you: towels. Unfold a towel over each drum, and it'll reduce the vibration when you hit it, which will make it a whole lot quieter. You can also fold a washcloth in half and tape it to your drumhead. Homemade solutions for making cymbals quieter are a little harder to come up with—but you can buy rubber muting pads for only about $6 to $10 each.

HOW TO PRACTICE

How you organize your band practice depends on how your band works creatively. Do you write by jamming together? Does one person write the songs and then teach them to everyone else? Do you each bring in different ideas to try? There is no one way to structure a band practice.

Band practice can be writing songs or parts, and then learning them, or it can be devoted to just figuring out one song. If you are practicing for a show, tour, or recording session, you will want to have practices where you just rehearse the songs over and over—no jamming, no writing, no reworking a part.

HOW TO BUILD A PRACTICE TENT

As with the baffle panels, you are channeling the sound in your room and giving it a direction. Here's how.

WHAT YOU WILL NEED:

★ Heavy blanket

★ Chair

★ Roll of masking or packing tape

★ Mic stand, the corner of a table, a mop (something to hold up the blanket)

1 Place your amp on a chair, facing you.

2 Lay the blanket over the amp and chair.

3 Tape the ends of the blanket to another chair or the wall so that the sound will be directed toward you.

4 Plug in and play.

THESE ARE THE BREAKS: THE RULES OF BAND PRACTICE

There are two rules for band practice. They are little things, but they make all the difference between having a productive practice and one that sucks. 1: Be on time. 2: Be prepared. The underlying principle is: *Do not flake on your band.* Even if something way more fun and exciting comes up or your crush

"We just love playing the shows! Some days you can feel tired, but as soon as you get on stage the energy runs and it's just amazing. If I come off the stage and I'm not pouring sweat I feel like I haven't done my job."

HALEY WILLIAMS, PARAMORE

wants to hang out—you've made a commitment, so there has to be a really good reason for missing a practice or showing up late (you are puking your guts out with the flu, or have to go to the hospital to get that shark bite treated).

Being prepared is showing up ready and able to do what you're expected to. Maybe that means knowing a new part to the song you are working on, having lyrics written, or bringing some song ideas. At the bare minimum, it means that all your equipment should be working, your instrument is tuned, and you have all the sticks, picks, or strings you need, plus some extras in case they break.

THE FINER POINTS OF BEING PREPARED

You love playing music and it's important to you, right? So treat it with love. That means, in addition to the things mentioined above, you should also 1) make sure to eat something before you go to practice so that you have neergy to put into playing, and 2) even if you have just had the worst day of your life at school, channel your frustration into your playing, not the other people in your band. The basics of being prepared stretch far beyond practices. They apply to that first show you play—and every one after.

Even if your band is an all-tambourine goof-around hobby band, these things show that you respect the other people in the band and their time. By taking these basic things seriously, you're also respecting your talent and your love of music. It sounds cheesy because it is—but it's also *totally true*!

Your practice schedule should reflect what's happening with your band. If you have stuff coming up (school talent show, MTV appearance, what have you), you practice more. Set a schedule and stick to it. Some members might be able to get together more frequently than you have scheduled—if you can, you should. I've been in bands where the rhythm section would get together and practice new songs between our regular practices, or the guitarists would get together and jam so that they wouldn't eat up entire practices noodling around. Practice as often as you have the opportunity to do so; you'll never look back and think, "Gee, I wish we'd practiced less for this show."

FEELING DISCOURAGED

Feeling discouraged is a natural part of making music. It's inevitable that one day, after tireless hours of practice, you'll feel like this just isn't worth it. In my first serious band, I constantly struggled to be able to play guitar the way I wanted to. I wanted to sound like my favorite guitarists and didn't. I had no idea how to make my hands do what I wanted them to. My frustration would've killed my desire to play if it hadn't been so much fun playing with my best friend (and if I hadn't wanted to be in a band so desperately). Fortunately, she felt my pain—we were both pretty new to playing and even when we were

Kaori Tsuchida and Ninja of The Go! Team.

really trying, we messed up all the time. If you are feeling stuck and aware of your beginner-ness, try playing with friends. It'll distract you out of your embarrassment—and you'll have a whole lot of fun!

You have to let go of any expectations you have about how fast you are going to get better. Yes, some musicians are born with a supernatural talent and write incredible songs without trying, but those people are freaks of nature. The

8 TIPS FOR BEATING THE BEGINNER BLUES

When the going gets tough, the tough sometimes have to take a breather. Here's some stuff to try when you start to feel crippled by your negative feelings about your own playing:

1 Step away from it and work on something else. Take a break for a day or two.

2 Write yourself a cheesy and encouraging note (with lots of exclamation points) and tape it to your guitar case or snare drum.

3 Listen to whatever songs or records inspire you the most and remember that there was once a time where the people in your favorite band didn't know how to play either.

4 Make a list of what you do know how to do. Every time you figure out something new, add it to the list.

I can:
* play without looking @ my hands
* play simple melody over 3 chords
* play & sing @ the same time

vast majority of people making music are regular-talented. All of those people, the untalented and the geniuses alike, do the exact same thing: They practice and they keep trying. There is only one way to NOT improve and that's to stop trying (I know, duh, but I had to say it). It's going to take as long as it takes for you to get good. There is no use comparing yourself to other people because it only makes you feel bad, which is unhelpful to the extreme.

The trio of misfit girls in *Ladies and Gentlemen, The Fabulous Stains* inspired a generation of female rockers.

6 Watch *Ladies and Gentlemen: The Fabulous Stains* (or another inspiring movie about being a girl in a band).

7 Eat a snack, take a walk around the block, fantasize about being onstage and ripping a complicated solo. Then return to your instrument.

8 Break down what you are doing into tiny parts. Rather than trying to figure out all of "Stairway To Heaven," just concentrate on mastering the first ten seconds. Do it one note at a time.

5 Remember that you are getting better with every practice—and then get back to work.

CHAPTER 3

RECORDING

There are several reasons why you should record your songs—the first and most important being FOR FUN. Documenting what you are doing—whether it's making up joke songs with your BFF or making your masterpiece of a first album—is a crucial part of your work as an artist. Recordings are the fruit of your labor; they're proof of your existence as a musician.

★★★

IS THIS THING ON?

The most basic reason for recording is posterity—simply so that you have a copy for later. It can be to help you remember how a song went or how things sounded in practice or keep track of ideas and first drafts as you hash out a song. Since the recording is for you or your bandmates, the quality of it isn't very important. As long as you can make out the notes you're playing or the words you're singing, it's fine. It's not *Cheap Trick Live at Budokhan*, it's *Becky Live from the Downstairs Bathroom*—it's a snapshot of a fledgling idea, to keep for your files. Get a little handheld recorder (digital or cassette), an old boom box at the thrift store for a few bucks, or use the recording software on your computer if you have one.

The other reason to make a recording is for people to hear it. This might be a demo that you use in order to book shows, it might be a record you sell, or for your MySpace page. You'll want the recording to be an accurate portrayal of what your band sounds like and the recording quality to be decent. It doesn't have to sound professional quality—no one expects that from a new, young band—but you don't want it to be, like, headache-inducing and so distorted that it sounds like you are flushing the microphone down a toilet. (There are exceptions to every rule: Noise bands, punk bands, and garage bands—the fans of those types of music are open to bad-sounding recordings. It's an accepted and encouraged part of those styles of music to make records that sound like you recorded in a dumpster.)

DO IT CLEAN

With a recording for other people to hear, you need to prepare. You need to practice. How much should you practice? Your options: a lot, often, or all the time. You should all be able to play the song in unison at the same speed without mistakes.

Genya Ravan of the pioneering girl group Goldie and the Gingerbreads was the first woman to produce a major label record.

There is some charm in rough, sloppy recordings, but your song being a mess is not the best way to showcase your talent. If you're recording in a studio or in another situation where you're paying someone to help, practice your butt off. Be as close to flawless as you can get. Practice till your pinkies are ready to fall off and you wonder why you ever thought starting a band was a good idea. Otherwise, you'll get into the studio (which is already a weird, nerve-wracking situation) and will waste time and money trying to get it right. Practice is free, whereas recording time in a studio starts at about $24 an hour. There are things you can fix with recording magic and technology, but there's no way to cover up bad playing. It's better to go in there and nail it rather than have your bandmates, the producer, and the recording engineer sit there and watch you fumble the chorus eleven times in a row.

Going into a studio with a producer and an engineer is the

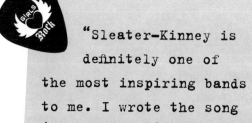

"Sleater-Kinney is definitely one of the most inspiring bands to me. I wrote the song 'Massive Cure' after we played with them, because I loved it how they rocked out so much and were so confident onstage."

ASYA, SMOOSH

professional way to record. If you have signed a recording contract with a record label, you'll probably be making that record in a studio. You don't need to start there. In fact, you really shouldn't. As a band that is just starting out, make demos on your own first. It's not worth spending money to have someone else record your band when you are still rough around the edges and developing your sound. If you make a studio recording when you're a brand new band, within a few weeks you're going to have new songs that you like better than what you just paid a bunch of money to

record. Develop your sound and your songs, and establish a fan base and a direction before you spend money on studio time.

BALLAD OF BIG SOMETHING: SETTING GOALS

What kind of recording you decide to do depends on what your goal is, and you need to know your goal. If you're recording just for fun and to document the songs you've written, you don't need to have a lot of concrete ideas. If you are making a proper record, however, you need to think about your approach and your overall sound. Make some preliminary, rough recordings of the songs you'd like to record, and listen to them a bunch and really study them. If there is "fat" (choruses that are too long and other parts that don't come together), you need to trim it now—rework the songs before you make your record. If you have a producer that you are working with, or another knowledgeable musician friend who is helping with your recording session, give them a copy of the rough

HIT THE BOOKS:
MUSIC HISTORY

Education and exploration of music history is essential. Here are some definitive guides that will break it all down for you.

Unsung Heroes of Rock 'n' Roll: The Birth of Rock in the Wild Years Before Elvis by Nick Tosches (Da Capo, 1999). One of the best music books ever written. Old blues players, weirdos you've never heard of and influential artists who helped shape everything that came along after.

Sweet Soul Music: Rhythm and Blues and the Southern Dream of Freedom by Peter Guralnick (Back Bay Books, 1999). This is THE classic book on R&B from its most important era (1950–1975). Musical and social history mixed with biographies.

Can't Stop Won't Stop: A History of the Hip-Hop Generation by Jeff Chang (Picador, 2005). Inspiring and compelling book about hip-hop in America, as a political, cultural, musical, and social force. It's a big-picture explanation of how music can affect and change society.

Our Band Could Be Your Life: Scenes from the American Indie Underground 1981–1991 by Michael Azerrad (Back Bay Books, 2002). Brief histories of the main indie bands of the 1980s and early '90s. A lot of information about the bands that

demos you've made. Go over it with them, listen together, and ask them for their input and ideas. Producers or a trusted friend can be helpful in pointing out things that could be improved, or could help come up with ideas that'll improve the final recording.

IT'S GONNA TAKE TIME ... A WHOLE LOT OF PRECIOUS TIME

In any recording situation, the main thing you need is patience. Everything is going to take longer than you think. Equipment has to get set up, microphones

influenced and shaped the underground. A little gossip, some greatness, and a lot of angry white guys with guitars.

Please Kill Me: The Uncensored Oral History of Punk by Legs McNeil and Gillian McCain (Grove Press, 2006). Oral history of the drugs, sex, and mayhem that was late '70s U.S. punk according to those who lived through it.

The Mansion on the Hill: Dylan, Young, Geffen, Springsteen, and the Head-on Collision of Rock and Commerce by Fred Goodman (Vintage, 1998). Covers the rise of the folk generation out of hippie coffee shops and onto the Woodstock stage, and follows rock as it turned into a corporate industry. One of the best books about the music business.

Funk: The Music, the People, and the Rhythm of the One by Rickey Vincent (St. Martin's Griffin, 1996). The best book on funk.

Rip It Up and Start Again: Postpunk 1978–1984 by Simon Reynolds (Penguin, 2006). The punk that happened after punk's first snarling, spitting wave. Lots of history, bands with keyboards and women in bands talking about how punk and music was changing their lives.

need to be arranged, knobs and levels need to be adjusted. Once everything is ready and you start playing, you'll find that things are very different than what you are used to. Songs won't sound like they do in your practice space. You'll be playing by yourself with headphones on while the engineer and your band watch you silently. Or the whole band might be playing at once, but the drummer will be in a separate room. It'll be a strange environment and a new circumstance; things will feel weird and formal even if it's just a home studio in someone's garage. It can be hard to relax and play normally when you know there are six people listening intently to your bass line.

Before you record, spend some time with your equipment. Take your guitar into the shop and make sure it's properly intonated, make sure your amp is not buzzing, and get new heads for your

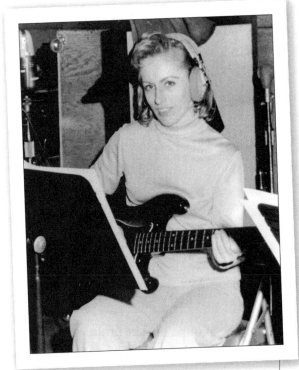

Carol Kaye is one of the most recorded musicians of all time; she played on hundreds of classic pop and rock songs of the '50s, '60s, and '70s.

drums. Take an hour to play by yourself and really listen to how your equipment sounds and make sure you are happy with it. Practice singing loudly by yourself. You don't want to wind up in the studio, listening to the playback and saying "Whoa, that's what I really sound like?"

If you don't have the interest or access to recording equipment, you'll have to find someone to help you record. Ask your other friends in bands or anyone who has a connection to music; it's not too hard to find someone with an eight track set up in their attic, or a little digital studio in their room. Before you commit to recording with someone, check out what else they've recorded and/or talk to musicians who've worked with them.

When you are considering a producer or someone to help you record, you want to make sure that they will be a good fit for what you want to accomplish. Some producers and studios only do electronic music, or only record commercials, rather than work with rock bands. Tell them how many songs you

"Record your stuff as live as possible—bass, two guitars, and drums. Keep that two-guitar thing going as long as possible. And keep it basic.... It's only in your own mistakes [that] you can find yourself."

**CHRISSIE HYNDE,
THE PRETENDERS**

want to do and ask how long they think it will take. If they tell you they can do it in one or two days, it's going to be bare bones and pretty rough.

Working with experienced professionals can be intimidating. Recording can be a mysterious process, so ask as many questions as you need to in order to understand. Don't worry about seeming naïve or inexperienced. Producers and engineers are used to working with new bands and it's in everyone's best interests that they

understand what you want and that everyone is on the same page. This also applies to once you actually start recording: If you don't know what you are doing or something doesn't sound right, speak up. It's better to look dumb for ten seconds than to spend two days recording with a bad sound mix in your headphones. The reason you work with a producer is so that you have someone you can trust to help you, so let them help.

HOW DO YOU KNOW YOU ARE READY TO RECORD?

My friends who work in studios tell me that many bands record prematurely; they aren't really ready, but they think that making a record will make other things suddenly happen for the band. Doing the things popular bands do (like recording in a fancy studio) will not make you a popular band. Spending a lot of money to record will not make your band any better than it is in real life. Recording in a studio doesn't mean you will suddenly get a record deal or better shows.

If you want to end up with a five-song recording, you should record seven songs. Record more songs than you need because then you have options; you aren't stuck with only those five. If you want to make a twelve-song album, have a few extras—that way, you can whittle down to the twelve best performances. If you've never recorded before and you have ten songs, pick the three that are well rehearsed—the ones that you know and play the best. It's better to do three songs really well than jam out ten not-so-perfect-ones as fast as you can.

If you are regularly playing shows, have a recording available. You can sell it, you can use it to get shows, or give them away to people who want to help your band out. If you are only playing a few shows a year, having a MySpace page is probably enough, and rough demos are fine. In fact, just having a MySpace page even if you are regularly playing shows will meet most of your band's needs.

YEARNIN', LEARNIN'

You learn a lot about recording by studying songs and how they sound. Before you get nuts with your solo recording, listen hard to the songs you love. How do they sound—are they slick and professional, or grimy and magical? How are they mixed—are there particular instruments that sound good together? How are they arranged—is it just a straight-ahead recording of the band or are there extra details like multiple tracks of the vocals or piano arrangements? What role does your instrument play in the types of music you love? How is it used differently in different genres?

ALL I NEED IS ONE MIC

When you are learning how to record, start with what is manageable: one microphone. You'll learn the most by learning how to get that one microphone placed properly and sounding decent.

GETTING THAT BONHAM DRUM SOUND

When I first started playing drums, I hated Led Zeppelin (I don't anymore), but I wanted my drums to sound just like John Bonham's. Many people will tell you that "the only way to get that Bonham sound is to be John Bonham." The dude was a total powerhouse freak of a drummer, and his stuff was recorded in an insane way that is virtually impossible to replicate (unless you have access to a castle)—but that's no reason to give up the dream.

Here are the specs on Bonham's drum kit:

★ Coated heads tuned medium high (medium tight)—almost jazz tuning

★ No pillows or anything muting the kick drum

★ 26-inch x 14-inch kick

★ 14-inch x 10-inch rack tom

★ 16-inch x 16-inch floor tom

★ 18-inch x 16-inch floor tom

★ 14-inch x 6.5-inch Chrome Supraphonic 402 Series Snare

Drummer John Bonham, playing his clear plastic Vistalite kit circa 1973.

Until you can do it right with one, it doesn't matter how many mics you have or how fancy they are. Get good with one, and you can move on to two, and eventually work your way up to artfully mic'ing a drum kit with five.

You can record with a single all-purpose microphone (Shure SM57), and get great results. For a digital mic, Blue Microphone's Snowball USB mic is decent, and doesn't cost much more than an SM57.

3

TIPS FOR MIC'ING DRUMS WITH ONE MIC

Now, using one mic when you're recording drums means you have less control of the sound—you can't turn the cymbals down and the kick drum up. Here are a couple of creative ways to make a one-mic setup work.

1 Install a plant hanger hook above your drums and hang a mic cable over it, so the mic is pointing down over your head. Adjust to where it sounds best and secure it with a piece of tape.

2 Drape it around your neck, securing the cord to your shirt with tape.

3 A few feet directly in front of your drums, aim the mic at your kit and align it with the top of your bass drum or a few inches lower.

YOUR EARS ARE YOUR BEST TOOLS

There are all kinds of funny little arrangements people use, but the best way to judge where to set the mic is to use your ears. Move around the room until you find where it sounds best. The mic will pick up the sounds similarly to how you hear them, so trust your ears.

RECORDING YOUR DRUM SOUND

If you play drums or play in a band with a drummer, you've learned that live drums don't sound like they do on your favorite albums. On a recording, they're deeper and fuller sounding—in your basement practice space, it's just harsh CHING! CHING! SNAP BOUFF BOUFF SNAP CHING! CHING! BOUFF. In most recording setups, a lot of "studio magic" is put on the drums. "Studio magic" is a joke term that means putting a ton of reverb and compression on a recording to change things from sounding flat and "blah" to something colossal and ultrapolished.

THE RINGO TWO-MIC SETUP

If you can get your hands on two mics, here's a foolproof setup that is sometimes referred to as the "Ringo setup" for The Beatles drummer who popularized it: Hang one mic about four feet directly above the kit, and then put another one a foot in front of the kick drum. For the budget approximation of the classic Beatles drum sound, throw T-shirts over your drums. They'll have a flat, soft sound but still be expressive.

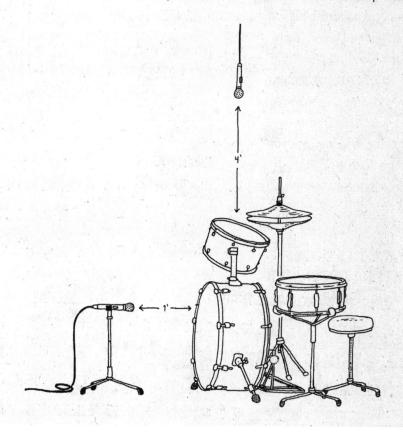

SPEED OF SOUND

The speed of sound is slower than the speed of light. How fast sound moves depends on how hot it is, but in a dry, room-temperature space, it goes roughly 300 meters (.02 miles) per second, or 700 miles per hour, or about five seconds per mile. The use of sound to measure distance and direction is called acoustic forensics, and it is an endlessly fascinating science. Acoustic forensics was used in investigations of the assassinations of President Kennedy and his brother, Robert Kennedy.

WHY YOU'D WANT TO RECORD IN THE BIGGEST ROOM POSSIBLE

A big room makes the drums sound big. Most rock drummers want their kits to sound bassy, deep, resonant—in a word, THUNDEROUS. The classic example of that big-boom drum sound is in Led Zeppelin's "When the Levee Breaks."

WHY YOU'D WANT TO RECORD IN A SMALLER ROOM

When you record in a large, boomy room, there is no way to make your drums sound smaller. Once they sound BIG, you can't shrink them. By recording in a small room (the vocal booth, a walk-in closet), you have a small-sounding recording that you can later adjust however you'd like.

HOW THE SHAPE OF THE ROOM CAN AFFECT THE RECORDING SOUND

In an empty box-shaped room, you are going to have "standing waves." Standing waves are a type of interference in the way that the room behaves with microphones that'll make things sound bad. It's better to record in a room that has stuff in it (your bedroom) because all those surfaces interrupt and deflect the sound waves. (See the diagram on page 94 for reference.)

PREPRODUCTION FOR RECORDING

"Preproduction" is a formal way of saying "preparing for the actual recording." It usually involves the producer (see right) sitting in on some

USING YOUR iPOD

You can record band practices or demo songs using your iPod and an iPod microphone. The Griffin iTalk is a cheap one (under $20) that records in stereo. If you are going to record with a full band, or record something loud, you're going to want to put the iPod on a surface that is far enough away that it isn't going to vibrate like crazy, or cushion it on someone's hoodie. You also might want to put something over it (like a mitten or a thick sock) to muffle the sound a bit, otherwise it'll come out sounding like BRRRRRRZZZZ. You'll have to mess around to find what's the best position for it in the room.

practices, making lists of additional gear or instruments you are going to need, suggesting arrangements of songs, and figuring out the schedule for when things will be recorded. Your job is to make sure the lyrics and music are firm, finished, and well rehearsed. If you want to add harmonies, samples, horns, or backup vocals on songs, you need to get those worked out before you go into the studio. If you aren't working with a producer, you will have to hammer out these details yourself.

WHAT IS A PRODUCER, AND DO YOU NEED ONE?

A producer helps pick out the best songs, gets the best performances out of the band, and motivates, critiques, and steers the process. They're thinking big picture—they help keep the recording on schedule and on budget and think about the record as a whole, so that all of the little details add up to what you are trying to build. Producers might produce every phase of your recording (basic tracks, overdubs, mixing) or just basic tracks and mixing.

PORTABLE STUDIOS

The Belkin Tune Studio iPod Recording Mixer, which sells for about $200, is like a digital version of the Tascam four-track, except it uses your iPod instead of a cassette. You can plug in both regular and USB microphones and it has ¼-inch inputs so you can go directly in with your guitar.

The BOSS MicroBR Digital Recorder, also about $200, is specifically for demoing songs. It's small enough to fit in your hand, you can record two tracks at the same time, and have up to thirty-two channels to play around with. It has a ¼-inch jack that you plug your instrument directly into, a built-in microphone, and a few hundred programmable beats that you can adjust and play along with. You can output the songs directly into your computer/iTunes.

PRODUCER SCHMODUCER! WHY AND WHEN YOU DON'T NEED ONE

If you are making a recording that is just for the band, or recording your live show, you do not need a producer. If you have never recorded before, and are recording in an informal situation (at a friend's house or in your garage), get a musician friend who has done some recording before to come by and help you. It's a good idea to have someone there who knows and understands what you are trying to do and has some experience recording. If someone in your band is a real whiz and understands the whole band's vision, she can produce.

Before I ever knew much about recording, I helped produce my friends' records. They trusted me, and I liked their music and understood what they were trying to do. I'd tell them what I thought sounded good or bad, or suggested "sing it again, but angrier," or "make the drums quieter." When you start recording, it's easy to lose perspective of what's good when you're doing the same part over and over.

You get in disagreements with your bandmates about who and what should be louder. A producer can simply be an extra set of ears that helps guide the project, someone who can be a sympathetic but impartial leader and can referee if needed.

WHAT IS AN ENGINEER?

Engineers set up the microphones and recording equipment and press record. They control the sounds you get on the recording. They sit behind the controls and adjust things; the producer usually bosses them around. They are involved in the entire recording process—basic tracks, overdubs, and mixing. The engineer's expertise and knowledge of how sound, mics, and the recording equipment works is what pulls the entire recording process together. Having an experienced engineer is essential to a polished, studio recording.

WHAT IS A MIXER?

The producer is usually the sound mixer, though sometimes you might have a mixer who is just a mixer and that's all that he or she does. Mixing is the final step in recording. When you have all the tracks to all the songs recorded, everything will be at the same level—the bass will be as loud as the vocals, etc., and it sounds raw and jumbled together. Mixing involves adjusting the levels of all the instruments—so the vocals and the drums are in their right place and the

SOME VOCAB

Overdubs: An overdub is anything that is recorded after your first initial track. It can be something that gets layered over the track—a solo, vocals, etc.—whether it's your second track or it's your 27th, it's an overdub.

Multitrack: A recording that has multiple recorded segments, which get combined together. A song you record using several channels on your four track is a multitrack recording. If you recorded a song that's just you playing guitar, and didn't add anything else after that, it'd be a single-track recording.

hi-hat and keyboard are not louder than the guitar. Mixing is the art of making your recording sound like a record, like something you want to listen to again and again.

IN THE BASEMENT: HOME RECORDING FOR THE SOLO ARTEEST

Some people say that "press record and go for it" is the only instruction you need for home recording. It really can be that simple. Recording solo involves figuring a lot of things out, stretching your creative boundaries and experimenting—it forces you to learn and adapt in ways that recording with a band, or in a studio, never will.

My friend Nora drums in a band, but last winter, she decided she wanted to make a solo record, on her own, in her bedroom. She borrowed a four-track recorder, a few microphones, and some instruments. She had little idea what she was doing—she just had lyrics and melodies worked out in her head. She called her friends who'd done home recording before and found that although they could explain how to plug things in and set up, everyone gave her the same advice: You figure it out as you go along.

While you may have musician friends or other resources (this book!) to lean on, home recording is one long show of self-reliance. When you play with a band or record with other

> "I moved in with a friend of mine from high school. She's a painter and [didn't] have a job, and I'd write music all day. Every time I stopped recording, I'd hear her downstairs singing along with me, which was horrifying, because it meant that she could hear everything I was doing. But then I realized I was making her a really big fan."
>
> **TEGAN QUIN, TEGAN AND SARA**

BEFORE YOU RECORD YOUR VOCALS

How you sing in practice and at shows is not how you sing when you are recording. In those first two places, you are singing to be heard above all the other sounds. When you are recording, usually, it's just going to be you, with some headphones on, alone in a room. It's only normal to feel bashful, but you have to confront that shyness and self-consciousness before it's time to record. Give yourself a few weeks to really get comfortable with your voice. Sing your songs until singing out loud and unaccompanied feels like no big deal. Or as close to no big deal as you can get. Also, don't eat dairy or drink anything cold before you do your vocals; they'll make your voice mucousy (ick).

people, you can use them and their skills to anchor what you are doing and give you feedback on what you are creating. Here you have to overcome any fear of going it alone and just trust your instincts. All you have are your opinion, your skills, your gear, and your mind. Any problems and solutions are going to be yours to handle. You are the only one who can decide if what you are doing is rad or not. Total freedom!

Home recording is about working with the defects, working with the mistakes, letting all the mistakes take over and being fabulous and weird. Maybe you're recording drums with one mic, and the drums are actually two buckets and a cookie sheet, so you have to just roll with it. Embrace all the stuff that seems like a mistake; embrace the simplicity of using that bucket-and-pan drum kit. Embrace that you are recording your solos in the laundry room while the cat uses the litter box. The way you decide to do things may not be the "right" way, but if you feel comfortable, then it is the best way to do it.

MICROPHONE TYPES

Dynamic Rugged, all-purpose mics that don't need phantom power (see box, right). They are good for mic'ing drums, bass, and live sound.

Ribbon Very smooth-sounding mics that don't need phantom power; good for mic'ing horns, acoustic guitars, and other acoustic instruments. They are so fragile that they have to be kept in a little padded case.

Condenser A mic whose durability varies and for which phantom power is needed. Best used for vocals and distance mic'ing.

PZM A very durable mic, ideal for mic'ing room sounds, drums, and piano. Must be placed on a large, flat surface to sound good—for example, the floor, wall, or a piano lid.

MOTHERS OF INVENTION

Be inventive and keep your ears open for the sounds you need. In a pro recording studio, the producer is going to be able to turn a zillion knobs and bring in five different snare drums to get the right sound. Maybe you don't have a kick drum and don't know anyone who does, so you're going to have to run the microphone out back and record yourself stomping on the porch. Or kick a cardboard box a few times and sample it. Try mic'ing any and all sounds that you can, and see what you come up with.

Recording solo also means really getting to know your gear, all of it, inside and out. Learn its complete range of sounds; twist all the dials into different configurations, try different tunings, beat your guitar strings with your dog's chew toy and then process the sound in GarageBand until it sounds like an underwater harp. By experimenting *a ton* before you start recording, you're going to know all your options. The other thing that all this messing around will show you is what your instrument/ gear/recorder won't (or can't) do. It forces you to figure out solutions ahead of time. You can also just choose to ignore the problem—which is a perfectly acceptable solution, too.

Working alone, you get to find out what your limitations are and adapt to them; the difficulties are going to force you to get inventive. By the end, you will be a lot less self-conscious about creating music and you'll also have recordings that are one-hundred percent you.

PHANTOM POWER IS NOT A GOTH METAL BAND

Some mics require something called "phantom power" in order to turn on; they don't have a power source built in, so they pull it from whatever they're plugged into. Most mics don't run on batteries. Some people believe that mics that run on batteries are not worth using, but that's just audio snobbery. You can get some awesome stuff out of battery-operated mics.

WORKIN' DAY AND NIGHT: FINISHING WHAT YOU START

The only thing to be wary of with home recording is that infinite quest to make what you are doing "perfect." Since there is no money or studio time involved, you can fix and refix and redo it differently and add some chimes and then add some other louder chimes. . . . And, suddenly, it's three months later, and you wake from your Rip Van Winkle–like creative state to find that you are still working on the same song and that you've pretty much tinkered it to death. Don't let what you are doing become a permanent work-in-progress rather than a finished album/song.

GARAGEBAND

GarageBand is the recording software that comes with Apple computers. One of the great things about it is that if you're cool with keeping things ultra-simple, you don't need any other equipment in order to record. You can use the built-in mic on your laptop and the virtual instruments in the software and start work on your triple album today. (For a complete tutorial, including how to mix and produce your GarageBand recording, see Appendix B at the back of the book.)

If you want to record live instruments or want a better mic to sing through, you have a few options: A cheapy USB mic costs about $30. They are for recording podcasts and aren't *ideal* for mic'ing a live instrument, but you totally can, it's just not going to sound great. A better/proper

INSTRUMENT CABLES AND SPEAKER CABLES: EVIL TWINS

Confusingly enough, speaker cables and instrument cables look exactly alike but can't be used interchangeably with each other. The main way to know the difference is that it's printed in tiny letters on the side of the cord. You can use an instrument cable as a speaker cable but not the other way around. If you confuse them, it won't blow up anything or wreck your guitar, it just won't sound like it should— you'll hear the difference.

mic for recording vocals and instruments is the Blue Snowball, which costs about $130. You are also going to need a decent pair of headphones (not earbuds). Get a pair of the over-ear kind that look like earmuffs, starting at around $30.

GANG OF FOUR: TASCAM FOUR-TRACK

Before there was GarageBand, there was the four-track. The Tascam four-track recorder was the standard in the pre-computer-magic era. The Tascam records on cassette tapes and four-track recordings sound raw and rock 'n' roll in a way that you can't duplicate with a computer. They cost $150 new ($250 for the digital, non-cassette model), but it's really easy to find used cassette models for $50 or less on your local Craigslist site (the instruction manuals are available online). It's perfect if you don't have a computer to record on, or if your equipment budget is limited. The downside is that you are recording on a cassette and when you're done, you can't instantly toss your latest anthem up on your MySpace page (unless you get the digital four-track). But what

A FOUR-TRACK MIND

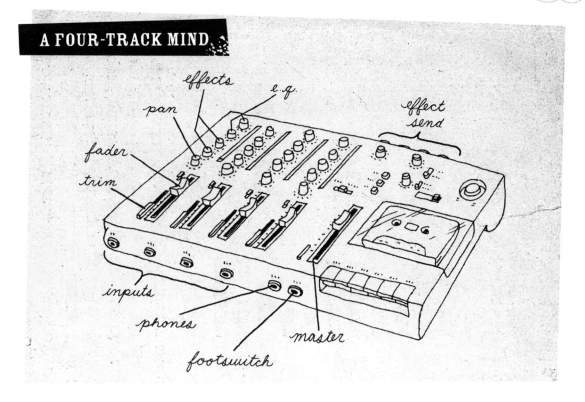

it lacks in being slick or computerized, it makes up for in every other way; it's low-tech, easy to find, and even easier to use.

GETTING TO KNOW YOU

Before you record, you should familiarize yourself with the parts and functions of your Tascam four-track.

★ EQ is short for Equalizer. There are two bands for each channel that you can adjust: low and high. Low frequency is bass, and high is the treble. There is no mid to adjust on Tascams.

★ PAN is also known as balance, you can adjust it to choose whether to send the signal to the left or right channel.

★ TRIM changes the volume in larger increments.

★ LEVEL / VOLUME FADER changes it in smaller increments; it's more like a fine-tuning volume knob for that individual channel.

★ MASTER changes the volume of all the channels at the same time.

★ INPUTS are the little silver sockets for ¼-inch instrument cable—you can plug your guitar/bass directly in, and the larger black sockets with three holes are XLR inputs for microphones.

★ EFFECT or EFFECT SEND knobs are for hooking up effects like reverb or delay (or any other kinds of stomp boxes or distortion pedals you have).

Once you get your four-track, you are going to need a mic and some cassettes to record on. Sixty-minute tapes are ideal; longer length ones are of lesser quality.

TO RECORD:

1 Arm the track by flipping the track arm switch all the way up to the number. Start with track one, and plug in your microphone or whatever instrument you are going to put on channel one.

2 Set the input switch to MIC/LINE; this allows whatever is plugged into that channel to be recorded.

3 Plug in and play a little, and adjust the trim and the fader so that the meter level is in the green, and not peaking in the red. Use the EQ to adjust the bass and treble.

4 Push the RECORD button down and then hit PLAY, and it'll start recording. If you adjust anything on the four-track while you are recording (EQ, volume) it'll record those changes.

5 Once you are done with that channel, set the recording arm switch to SAFE, which will keep it from getting recorded over.

Record each track in order—start with one, then go to two, and then three. To play along with the previous track(s) you've recorded, change the previous track's input to "Tape." Plug in your headphones to hear whatever you have recorded already and play along (this is called overdubbing). The fader controls the playback volume. Make sure that, in the monitor section, the L-R button is depressed. Now, record like you did on the previous track and so on until you finish with track three.

Once you have three tracks, you are going to use track four to "bounce down" (also called ping-ponging)—you take the sound that is on the first three tracks and combine and mix them onto the fourth track.

FOUR-TRACK MIX-DOWN

After recording the song to tape, you want to mix down:

1 Set all the track inputs to Tape.

2 Make sure the L-R monitor button is depressed/pushed in.

3 Set your levels.

4 Use the volume, pan, and EQs to create your mix.

Also, if you have some effects pedals, you

> "There are moments when the tech masters me and it's totally hilarious. I'm really into making a mistake on the sampler and then building on that."
>
> **KATHLEEN HANNA, LE TIGRE/BIKINI KILL**

can add those into your mix by hooking them up to the four-track:

1 Going out of the top of the recorder, run a ¼-inch instrument cable from EFFECTS SEND 1 to the IN jack on your pedal.

2 Run another cable from the OUT jack on the pedal back into the recorder and INPUT 5 and 6 or 7 and 8. Now, you are filtering the sounds you have recorded through the effects pedal, and making it part of the mix. Reverb, delay, or echo pedals can make your mix a little sweeter and warmer sounding.

MASTER COPY-MAKING

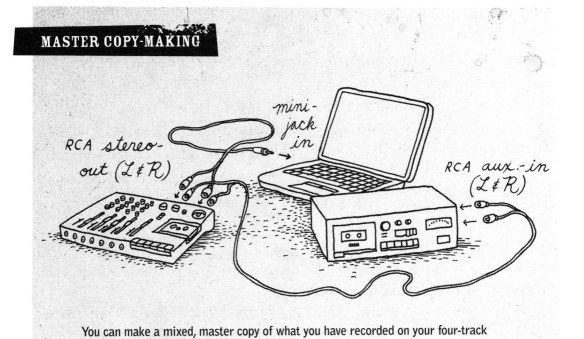

You can make a mixed, master copy of what you have recorded on your four-track using a stereo or a computer.

3 Adjust how much sound you are sending with the EFFECTS SEND knob and the EFFECTS RETURN knob. This determines how much of what you recorded is going through the effects box, and how much you want to hear that effect in the final version of the song.

A final "master" copy needs to be recorded on something else—a stereo tape deck, a computer, etc. You won't be able to just play your cassette recording as is. To make your master copy, refer to the diagram above. First, run a stereo RCA cable from the four-track's output into your tape deck or computer. Press "record" on that external gear, and then press "play" on the four-track. Press "stop" on both machines when the song is finished. You now have a master copy of the mixed song.

TIPS 'N' TRICKS FOR THE FOUR-TRACK

1 Adjust the pitch control when you are recording your guitar. If you record while the pitch is at the lowest speed, when you play the track back, what you recorded will be faster and higher pitched. If you record at a faster speed, what you've recorded will sound lower and slower when played back at regular speed. This is useful if you are making heavy, atmospheric music (black metal), or for your vocals if you want them to sound deeper or, um, manly.

2 When you are recording a song, start by recording the drum tracks first, the guitar/bass/keys next, and the vocals last.

3 Always tune your guitar before you record a song. Tune it using a tuner, not to the guitar itself.

MINI-INFO ON MIDI

"MIDI" is a signal that a keyboard uses to talk to the recording program in your computer. It's not a sound—you couldn't plug into an amp and make a sound using MIDI. MIDI is like this: On a regular computer typing keyboard, when you type the letter G on the keyboard, a G shows up on the screen. MIDI works the exact same way except you assign a sound (e.g., a violin or a drum beat) instead of letters. Basically, you are typing a sound and the sound is manufactured digitally inside the computer program.

CHAPTER 4

ALL THE WAY LIVE

There is no exact way to figure out when it's the right time to take your band from the private confines of your practice space and into the public eye. I've been in bands that formed in order to play a show three days later. I've been in bands where we practiced three times a week for a year and a half before playing for an audience. It depends on what your standards are for your own performance, how serious you are about your band, and what the other band members want.

★★★

READY, STEADY, GO

Being in an impromptu party band is super fun. I recommend you try it at least once. If you or your friend is having a party or house show, form a band for the party. Practice at least twice, come up with a few songs, and maybe learn a cover or two. (A "cover" means playing a song written by someone else. "Louie Louie," The Stooges' "I Wanna Be Your Dog," and The Troggs' "Wild Thing" are easy songs with only three chords, and standards for party bands.) The main thing you have to deal with is your own expectations; your performance could be sixteen minutes of messy genius

(probably), or you could be laughing so hard you can't finish singing the song that you barely remember how to play in the first place. Whether it's amazing

"To me, being in a band is about more than just playing our music and leaving. It's also about reaching out to our fans, making connections with them, building relationships."

CHAUNTELLE DUPREE, EISLEY

or amazingly bad, putting together a last-minute band will help you get over any stage fright you might have. There's no place for embarrassment in this situation. You aren't trying to be perfect. You are trying to be loud, funny, and get your friends to dance. Any and all band experiences you have are valuable, so play a show for eleven people in a toolshed—and don't sweat your technique.

That said, if you are playing in a serious band and trying to build a serious reputation: Don't play shows until your band sounds solid. How long that takes is different for every band. It may take six months for your band to write ten decent songs, and then another six months of diligent practicing. It might be another three months on top of that before you can get a show. Or it might only take two months to feel ready because you're out of school for the summer and you spend eight hours a day practicing.

DRESS REHEARSAL RAG: GETTING READY FOR YOUR SHOW

Rehearsing for a show is different than regular old practice. First, there are the getting ready practices, which should involve the following:

1. Play every song your band has.
2. Pick out the songs you play best.
3. Pick out the songs that are the most fun to play.
4. Make a list of those best-played and most fun songs.

The songs on the list are going to be what you play at your show. Organize this list into a *set list* for your show by playing them in different orders to see what songs sound good after one another. Think about what mood or direction you want for your set. Are you going to start with all the slow songs first and get progressively louder? Do you want to put the catchiest song first to get people's attention? Do you want to alternate between slow and fast songs? Do you want to save all the danceable ones for a big finale at the end of the set?

If you have songs that are in alternate tunings, or require special equipment or involve switching instruments, clump those songs together so that you don't tune and detune, or stop between songs to move a xylophone around the stage. If you have two guitars, you can have one in your special tuning and one in your regular tuning and you can switch between them as you need to. While the point of playing live is expressing yourself to other people, it's also about connection. You're trying to connect with your audience, inspire and entertain them. It doesn't matter how brilliant your songs are, if there are long pauses between songs, you will lose the audience's interest fast.

You can't take their interest for granted, unless the whole audience is your dad, best friend, and your grandma. There is an unspoken deal between a performer and her audience: We paid to see you, please at least try to entertain us. If they sense you're trying (even if you aren't succeeding), they will be polite. Otherwise, if they think you are taking their attention for granted, they may complain loudly that they should have saved their $4 and stayed home and watched *America's Next Top Model*.

WHAT? MORE PRACTICING?

So, let's say you've had a couple practices and have determined what songs you are going to play and in what order. You can now move into Official Phase Two of the Getting Ready

Tina Weymouth, mega-influential bassist of Talking Heads, was once a cheerleader.

> "[My album, *Exile in Guyville*] was a very clear reaction to what I was exposed to over and over again. It was definitely designed to take a crack at the male norm of rock 'n' roll. I was definitely swinging away at that piñata."
>
> **LIZ PHAIR**

Practices. In these practices, you are going to pretend you are playing your live show, like so:

1 Set up how you will be set up on stage. Face the imaginary audience, rather than each other. You have to learn not to depend on visual cues. You need to know when the break in the chorus happens and not rely on the bassist winking at you to get it right.

2 If, for some reason, you normally sit during band rehearsals, stand up. Unless you play a sit-down instrument or have a good excuse.

3 Time how long it takes you to play through your whole set, each time you play it.

4 Play through your set without stopping no matter who screws up or how badly. This has to do with timing, but also with being prepared for a real show.

5 Partway through your set, check that your guitar is in tune. Practice tuning at home so that you can do it quickly (in under a minute).

6 If your show involves costumes, costume changes, projections, puppets, props, or large-scale weirdness, have at least one full dress rehearsal.

7 Have at least five of these practices in the weeks before your first show.

SING ANOTHER SONG, GIRLS

You should have these kinds of practices until you get to the point where the whole band is playing the whole set correctly, back-to-back-to-back songs, without any major mess-ups. Once you get to the point where you can do that, do it a few more times. Take a break and do it again *all the way through*. Don't do it more than, say, twenty times, though. It'll kill the vibe and you'll hate the songs. Also, don't make changes to the songs a few days before the show. If you feel a song needs a major overhaul, either cut it from the set or make the changes after you've played the show. Don't go switching stuff around right before the show because one of you will forget.

Practicing your exact set so many times sounds boring, but strangely

enough, it isn't. The more you play, the more accomplished and rad you'll feel. You'll exchange a look with your bandmate that says, "We are nailing this." And when you're done, you'll feel invincible.

The reason you're going to practice like maniacs for that first show is so that you know, in your brain, that you can do this. You might feel golden with confidence in the last practice before the show. Then, once you get onstage, your hand is shaking so bad it looks like an affliction and your heart is pounding and you feel like you are going to puke all over the drums with nervousness. Your brain is going to have to reason with your nerves and your heart, and the main ammo it has is: "Remember, you played this ten times through perfectly last week, you can do it again, here in this basement with nineteen people watching." Or maybe

Mika Miko formed while they were all still in high school.

you practiced so much you are only regular nervous, and the show is a breeze.

Practicing hard may not make you 100 percent confident, but it will give you some confidence. All you need is *some*, just enough to propel you onto the stage, and then you force it from there. You play your way through the fear. The more you perform in front of other people, any mistakes you make become less and less of a big deal. That's how everyone does it. And if you do actually puke, don't sweat it, because years later, when you're sitting backstage talking to other musicians about your worst-show horror stories, you will always win with, "I opened my mouth to sing and projectile vomited on the entire front row at our first show."

SOME NOTES ON STAGE FRIGHT AND BAD SHOWS

Stage fright, for many performers, never goes away. After thousands of shows, they get at least a little nervous before they go onstage. It is important to accept it and just observe what's happening. "Wow, my hands are shaking really bad and I'm playing the song twice as fast as it's supposed to go. Okay then. Next song." This is better than just feeling bad about it.

If you feel really shaky and inadequate, try to bring yourself back to the thought that you are proud of the music you have made and concentrate on the fact that you are sharing it with people. *And* it's just a show. Just one show of the hundreds or thousands of shows you are going to play.

If you do mess up, and especially if you mess up big—what comes after that is usually a really awesome show. Believe it. Mistakes can make an audience really love you—because it's a reminder that you are normal like them and you and everyone in the room just shared this funny little moment together. Plus, it's never, ever as bad as you think it is.

Something you'll find out after you have been playing shows for a while is that there is no such thing as a good show, or a bad show. There will be times where you get offstage thinking "How are these people still standing?! We just tore this place apart!" And your friends will be like, "Yeah, I guess it was pretty okay." Or you'll play a show that you thought was exceptionally flat and person after person will tell you how blown away they were. How it feels for you and how it feels for the audience can be wildly different. It's not really part of your job to judge whether you played a good or bad show. It's your job to show your art to the audience and see what happens.

> "You have to be ready for anything, because while you're onstage, the fans can be really unpredictable. Stuff is hurled at you. You'll be in the middle of a song and they'll come up to the lip of the stage demanding you sign some piece of paper. And you'll be like, 'Uh, well, I'm actually a little busy right now!'"
>
> **NANCY WILSON, HEART**

Heart's biggest hit, "Barracuda," was written in response to an interview with a sexist music journalist. The song went to No. 11.

I WAS MEANT FOR THE STAGE

What *is* stage presence? It's being connected to what you are doing. It's a combination of confidence, engaging the audience, and really being into what you are doing. When you are up onstage, it's easy to zone out in other thoughts like, "I've played this song 112 times this month," or "That's a cool dress she has on," or "I bet they hate this." Here are some tips for stage presence:

★ **Look people in the eye.** Pick someone. You don't need to stare them down Firestarter style. Just a glance is fine. This is better than just staring over their heads.

★ **Dedicate yourself to the lyrics** as you sing them. Remember what the song is about and why you wrote it and really put all those emotions behind whatever is coming out of your mouth.

★ **Don't ham it up.** The desire to ham it up comes from being afraid that you aren't being entertaining enough. (The exception to this is, of course, if you are in a hammy band, joke band, or other type of goofball ensemble where

> "I try not to think too much about what the audience is thinking and what they think I should do. I'd be self-conscious if I did. Anyone becomes mannered if you think too much about what other people think."
>
> **KIM GORDON, SONIC YOUTH**

your whole performance hinges on hamminess.)

★ **Stay in your own head and keep your focus** on what you are trying to do, rather than supposing what the audience is thinking.

As a performer, you have to be able to command the audience. Rock 'n' roll is about swagger and confidence—and that's not a dude thing, that's a rock thing. It's as much your right as any guy who gets on the stage after you. When you are playing, you're the boss of the ship, and what sort of confidence you show determines whether that ship is going to sink or sail.

Be ambitious and audacious—the people watching you will appreciate your sense of adventure even if things don't go as planned. If you do mess up, don't show you messed up by mouthing "Oops!" and wincing with embarrassment. Unless your audience knows all your songs by heart, they probably won't know you hit a wrong note. If you screw up, just keep playing, don't start over or apologize—it interrupts the flow of the action. Mistakes are not a big deal. You are not Celine Dion, this is not some Vegas show palace, and no one paid $200 to get front row at your show. Audiences trust that whatever is happening onstage is part of the show unless you tell them otherwise.

While you can't wish your stage fright or nervousness away, just try not to show it to your audience. If you are afraid you are going to say something stupid, simply say "Thanks" after they applaud your song, and "Goodnight" when you end your set. Focus on what you're sharing with the audience rather than the soul-quaking panic you're feeling inside. Being consumed by the fear that you are about to mess up, or worrying that the lights make your head look fat will take away from the intensity of the performance. The goal of playing shows isn't "getting it right"; it's self-expression (and if you are ambitious, entertainment). People don't want to see some perfect robot; people want to hear life reflected in a song. They want to forget that they just spent all day trimming Labradoodles at the dog grooming place, they want to believe in the true love you are singing about, or they want to dance all night to your jams. The more fun you have with what you are doing, the more an audience will connect to your songs.

HECKLERS

If you get heckled by someone, you don't have to respond. Ignore it, and know that the rest of the audience thinks the heckler is a jerk. That said, if the heckler is particularly rude, and if you think of a good comeback, let it rip. Beware though, that like in any schoolyard throw down, it might just up the ante.

ONE IS THE LONELIEST NUMBER: PERFORMING SOLO

Going solo is a whole other ballgame. The risk in performing solo is that if you mess up or the audience hates it, there aren't other people to share in that (or blame it on). Your mistakes and embarrassments are yours alone. But since you are endeavoring on such a daring act, there is no reason to do anything less than *exactly what you want to do*. Whatever it is you spend a lot of time in your mind planning and fantasizing about—that's what you need to explore. Especially if you think "I could never do that." That's precisely the music and idea you need to put on full blast. Seriously. Being solo is your opportunity to be as elaborate, personal, savage, silly—and loud—as you want without compromise. Why bother getting onstage or recording your songs unless they are absolutely you and from your guts? Being a solo artist, for all its freedom, requires discipline. After all, you are the focus of the audience's attention—which can turn even the coolest lady into a

> "I've got an overwhelming desire to sing and play music, particularly to people. I don't feel like I'd even be living out my role on earth if I didn't do it."
>
> **PJ HARVEY**

sweaty-palmed wreck. There is no one else's guitar solo to hide behind, so you have to practice until you are really confident with your songs. You don't have to be flawless, but you should play and play until the song feels easy and instinctual—like you could do it with your eyes shut. If you know your songs inside and out, you are going to be able to relax and be self-assured in your performance (I know, easier said than done).

Since there's not a full band onstage, there is a certain amount of space you have to fill. Not physical space—you don't have to cartwheel around your bass amp—but you must have "presence." You have to get up there and be brave, resisting the urge to shrink up and be shy. Walk onstage with confidence and a clear idea about what you're doing and why. If you present yourself like you have a clear purpose, people will give you their full attention, even if they hate music and think your outfit is heinous. If you get onstage and announce that you are nervous, apologize, or say that things might suck before you even start, the audience will take this as a warning. It's as if you are prescribing them not to care. If you're well practiced, passionate, and seem like you believe in what you are doing, the audience will believe, too.

THE SYSTEM AND THE PACKER WHO ABIDES BY IT

It's good to have a system for packing up. This way, you won't leave anything behind after your show. Using your colored duct tape, affix a little tape square on every case, amp, or box of stuff and number it. In your band-business folder and taped up in your car or van (however you get to and from shows),

SING A SIMPLE SONG: HIGH CONCEPTS FOR THE SOLO BABE

Keep the potential for messing up low by not getting too super complicated. Conceptual stuff— multiple costume changes, barking raps from your puppy Charles, a PowerPoint presentation—is awesome, but when your performance is rife with big ideas, you want to avoid having a really elaborate setup, where, if one thing goes wrong, the whole set is a lost cause. Switching among three or more instruments, or a lot of tuning or setup, is not a good idea. It's essential to think big and hatch big plans, but anything that is going to create long, dead minutes between your songs is going to bum your audience out. Streamline your performances so you can transition easily between songs. Recruit a friend to assist you so you don't have to wheel the papier-mâché volcano onstage by yourself. That way, you can just turn around and climb in it (or whatever).

A CHECKLIST FOR YOUR FIRST SHOW (AND EVERY SHOW AFTER)

FOR THE WHOLE BAND

- ☐ All equipment is in working order
- ☐ You can take apart and set your gear up properly in a reasonable amount of time

FOR GUITAR/BASS

- ☐ Extra full set of strings
- ☐ At least a half dozen guitar picks. Put some in your case and some in your pocket.
- ☐ Guitar cable
- ☐ Guitar strap
- ☐ Guitar
- ☐ Guitar case
- ☐ Tuner
- ☐ Amp
- ☐ Pedals
- ☐ Cords for pedals/tuner
- ☐ String winder
- ☐ Extra, fully charged batteries for your pedals and tuner

- ☐ Miscellaneous accessories (capo, slide, wire cutters)

FOR DRUMS

- ☐ Drums
- ☐ Hardware
- ☐ Cymbals
- ☐ Three sets of sticks
- ☐ Tuning key
- ☐ Brushes/mallets/maracas (if you use them)
- ☐ Pillow/blanket for inside your kick (if you use it)
- ☐ Cinderblock or drum rug to keep your drums from scooting (If you drum hard, your drums will scoot forward; if you are playing at a club, they'll probably have something, but at other places you will probably need to bring your own.)

FOR SINGERS

- ☐ Mic cover (if you use one, and you should, unless you bring your own mic)

- [ ] Attitude
- [ ] Energy
- [ ] Cool outfit
- [ ] Tambourine/harmonica/maracas (if you use them)

FOR KEYBOARDS

- [ ] Keyboard
- [ ] Power adapter
- [ ] Cables
- [ ] Spare cable
- [ ] Spare power adapter

EXTRAS

(Basic Stuff Your Band Should Have on Hand)

- [ ] Roll of strong duct tape or cloth gaffers tape
- [ ] A marker
- [ ] Two spare nine-volt batteries
- [ ] Four AA batteries
- [ ] Box of Band-Aids

- [ ] Towels and change of clothes (if you sweat a lot)
- [ ] Earplugs (enough for everyone in the band and extras)
- [ ] Spare instrument cable

OFFICIAL STUFF

- [ ] Directions to venue
- [ ] Copy of your contract for the show (if there is one)
- [ ] Phone number for venue
- [ ] Phone number for promoter/booker
- [ ] Way to get to the show

MERCH TABLE

- [ ] T-shirts
- [ ] CDs or whatever music you have to offer
- [ ] Clipboard with e-mail list sign-up
- [ ] Stickers
- [ ] $20 in ones, or whatever you need to make change for what you're selling

have a corresponding list of all your band's items. This way, you can just count off. Someone has to be responsible for double–checking (doing a "dummy check") and arranging the equipment as you pack it into the van. Try it a few ways and have a diagram of how it best fits in. Have the diagram taped up with the equipment list so it gets done right. Haphazard packing will almost always result in damaged equipment (or someone's stuff being left backstage).

The Go-Go's were the first all-female band that played their own instruments and wrote their own hit songs.

PUTTING ON YOUR OWN SHOWS

Here's the secret about shows, which seems like a no-brainer, but it's so easy to work this to your band's advantage: You can play a show *anywhere*. Anywhere, except maybe a plane. If you are even the teeniest bit resourceful (you are) and ambitious (ditto), you can pull together the coolest shows and music experiences that your fans will remember

their whole life long. YES, THEIR WHOLE LIVES.

Any ol' band can book a show at the crappy/cool rock club in town—and that's what most bands want to do. They want to play the same place all their favorite bands play. And if that's what you want, too, that's fine. Many of the bands I've been in wanted to play shows at the cool club, so we could work up to playing at the cooler club, and eventually play the big venue with the lights and high stage and two thousand

"When I saw that [Led Zeppelin opening for The Who], believe it or not, an eleven-year-old girl said to herself at that point, 'This is what I want to do.' That was it, it changed everything for me, everything. We went to see them at Meriweather Post Pavilion, and among one of the most memorable, biggest thrills of my life is that, eleven or twelve years later, I actually got to play on that stage."

GINA SCHOCK, THE GO-GO'S

a truck, in a library, in a living room (the list goes on and on)—those are the kinds of shows I remember and still talk about. And as someone who has played shows in a Chinese restaurant, an Elks Lodge, and an abandoned half-built factory—that is the special stuff where when you get done you think, "This is why I'm in a band." You feel a much more intense sense of community and friendship and adventure than you do playing at traditional venues (clubs and bars). You can have those connections and feelings at clubs, but it's different when your friends are showing up early to help carry your drum kit a mile to the beach.

The other reason that alternative venue ideas are important to consider is because as a young/new band, you might not be able to get a show at the regular places. Which means that if you want to play, you're going to have to make it happen for yourself. The other factor is, if you live in a small or rural town, there might be only one venue and it's a random cowboy bar out by the highway. You want to stick to playing places that are appropriate. Organizing parties and

screaming people. There is nothing wrong about wanting to take that path. You can be on that path *and* do surprise shows at the Laundromat; it's not a one-or-the-other deal.

As someone who has gone to shows on rooftops, in the woods, in the back of

PLACES TO PUT ON YOUR BAND'S SHOW

Depending on your technical requirements, you can have a show any place where there is space to set up and a couple working power outlets. Here are a few ideas, in no particular order:

★ Pizza joints

★ Coffee shops

★ Ice cream shops

★ Churches

★ School dances

★ Your garage

★ Someone else's garage

★ Any place with a skate ramp. If there is a half pipe, it means they want a show. This is common knowledge.

★ A drained swimming pool

★ A boat

★ A little boat that you could tie up to a dock or pull up on the beach

where people could meet you and watch and listen (if your band is acoustic)

★ Hotel lobby

★ Parking lot

★ Parking garage

★ A tent

★ A cul-de-sac on a residential street

★ A patio

★ Your room

★ A basement

★ The library

★ A roller-skating rink

★ An ice-skating rink

★ The cultural affairs building

★ A gazebo in the park

★ In the park or on an available grassy knoll

★ A loading dock

★ Any place safe where there is electricity

★ The back of a flatbed truck

★ In a van

★ Wherever you work

★ Art gallery

★ Nursing home

★ Record store

★ Bookstore

★ Doorway

★ Sidewalk

★ Community center

- ★ Practice space

- ★ On or under a bridge (as long as it's well lit and safe)

- ★ Your backyard

- ★ Inside a super structure you build out of thirty-one cardboard boxes and a parachute

- ★ The old movie theater in the daytime, or late at night

- ★ Small theaters or wherever they have puppet shows in your town

- ★ Farmer's market

- ★ A barn

- ★ School gymnasium (just a warning: the sound will be pretty bad)

- ★ A college (lots of colleges have venues, call the college radio station and ask for info if you don't know)

- ★ Sorority house

- ★ Elks hall

- ★ Large toolshed

- ★ Bowling alley

- ★ VFW hall

- ★ VA hospital

- ★ Local geodesic dome

- ★ Museum

- ★ Bat/Bar mitzvah

- ★ On a trampoline

- ★ Playground

- ★ Campground

- ★ Summer camp

- ★ On a parade float

- ★ Inside a house/building, next to open windows, and have everyone sit on the curb across the street (I saw a show like this and it was great)

A gazebo in the local park could be the perfect stage for your next show.

shows in order for your band to play rather than just waiting to get on to a show at the club every other month is the best thing you can do.

My friend Kate started a band when she was eleven and the only spot they could get a show booked was a pizza place by her house. All their friends showed up and, naturally, ordered pizza. Of course, the pizza place was into that, so they hired them to play every Friday night. Her band kept playing there, every weekend, *for three more years.* They were an instrumental, all-girl band who were all still in junior high, and the restaurant eventually painted a mural of them on the wall. By the time they were all fourteen and fifteen, they were too popular to play there anymore.

They were playing other shows all over town, opening for huge bands, and playing to thousands of people. So, as you are loading in your gear through the back door of Edna's Shrimp 'n' Subs (downtown location), and you find yourself wondering, "Where is playing to these eleven shrimp-eating people going to get me?!" remember that opportunities can happen anywhere, and you never know exactly what could be the catalyst for greater things.

If you're open-minded and determined, *any* place is an option as long as you make sure that it's safe and you aren't going to get arrested for playing there.

1 Playing in an abandoned factory on the outskirts of town may seem like a good idea, but a steel beam could be about to fall from the ceiling or there could be creepy people camped out there, so it's better to go with places you know are going to be okay.

2 Don't play any place where there are animals (either captive or loose in the wild) because they have sensitive ears.

3 Don't play any place where there are a bunch of (or *any*) elderly people around, unless you have been invited to play a nursing home, or your grandma is letting you have a show in her garage. Old people will call the cops immediately and your show will get shut down before you can finish the first song.

WELCOME TO THE WORKING WEEK: D.I.Y. EFFORTS

You have to put a little more effort into having a DIY show someplace that doesn't normally have music. Because there is a much better chance of things going wrong, take care of as much as you possibly can on your own, in advance.

You will need some sort of P.A. (public address) system. In a club setting, the P.A. is a series of big speakers connected to the soundboard and microphones, and is amplifying every part of the band, for both the band and audience. In a little setting, you don't need that stuff, nor do you want to be renting and hauling a giant P.A. to the picnic table stage behind the Dairy Queen (or wherever). In the non-venue spot, your P.A. is going to be an amp or speaker for someone to sing out of. Borrow

No Age used a small portable generator to play a show in the LA River basin.

out a small amp. But if you can't come up with extra equipment, go with what you have. A practice amp is probably going to be fine (unless you have an exceedingly large or exceedingly loud band).

You'll need a roadie or two. When you get to a rock club, there is usually a staff person and/or a sound person who will help set things up or maybe help you load your equipment in. They don't have those people at the skate park/grain silo/VFW hall, and you'll need an extra set of hands—someone you can send to grab the thing you forgot. Ask a handy friend who can take (friendly) direction and has any/some working knowledge of how a show is supposed to go down (loan her this book if she doesn't).

You're responsible for the promotion for your show—it's up to you to get the word out. At a club, there is someone who is paid to put up posters, handle advertising, and other publicity. If

one, or sometimes you can run a mic through a bass head/speaker if it has an extra jack. It's better to get a separate amp/cab to sing through, so you don't blow

you are playing at a Quonset hut at a campground, there is no promotions department there to handle that. A rock club does shows a couple nights a week, so people will go there knowing that a show will be happening—not the case with, say, the beach. If you want people to come to your show at the unconventional spot, you have to promote it well.

SHOW-STOPPER

Make sure you're legal. You want to stick to places where you have the permission of whoever owns the space. Don't do shows if it involves trespassing. The last thing your band needs is a tangle with the law (though if this happens, I suggest you call your first album *Juvenile Record*). If you are doing shows in a residential area make sure the neighbors know and are cool with it. Let them know a band will be playing, tell them what time the party/show starts and ends (and make sure you stick to that schedule), and if you are nice and polite and smile big and tell them thank you, they aren't going to call the cops. Be mindful of noise

and use common sense. Don't play a super loud two-hour set with your amps pointed right at their house late on a weeknight. If it's your friend's barn in the middle of nowhere, go ahead and invite your four hundred closest friends. If you are playing someplace that can only fit twenty people, don't invite more than thirty people. If you are playing someplace where people could easily and quickly be bothered by the noise you are making, play a thirteen-minute set, so that you can be done before anyone gets annoyed enough to call the cops.

"I'm absolutely certain that the love that comes back at you from an audience is one of the things that keeps you going—totally. But you can always play music, irrespective of your age or the size of your audience."

DEBBIE HARRY, BLONDIE

If you are playing a show at a business (store, restaurant, lumberyard), when you set up the show, make sure you discuss with the manager (or whomever you are arranging things with) what the deal is. Who is responsible for cleanup? Are you getting paid, or is what you make based on a percentage of how many sandwiches they sell while you play? Are you getting paid in sandwiches? How long are you expected to play for? What time do they want you to start and end? When you play a regular club, they have a particular, official way of doing things. At the lumberyard, this may be the first show they've ever done, so you'll have to hash it out a bit.

RIGHT HERE, RIGHT NOW

Another idea is to find a working outlet at the base of a light post by the field house in the park, tell eleven of your friends to meet you there at 4 P.M. on Sunday. Drag your practice amp down and play a blazing fifteen-minute set of your new songs. It doesn't have to be a big production.

If you play something you can play quietly (like an acoustic instrument, sorry drummers!), you can have a show pretty much anywhere there is room for a few people to sit/stand. You can perform on the curb in front of your house, to whomever happens to be passing by. People are going to be stoked. They will stop and call their friends and tell them they have to come down to Thirteenth and Elm and check out this girl playing Radiohead songs on her harmonica. (I'd ride my bike three or four miles to see something like that.)

There is a lot of traditional thinking about what rock is and how it is played, by whom and why. It's expected that, as a musician, you will start out playing parties, move on to clubs and bars, the whole time hoping that eventually you move on to playing big theaters or stadiums. It's expected that the only way to reach a lot of people is to make really simple, regular pop music, which is barely true.

Here's the thing: You can do all of it however you want, especially when

HIT THE BOOKS:

DIG IF YOU WILL A PICTURE...

They say that a picture is worth a thousand words. Here are five must-read—and must-*see*—books that document rock's rich history in all its glamour, glory, and grit.

The Rolling Stone Illustrated History of Rock and Roll: The Definitive History of the Most Important Artists and Their Music by the editors of Rolling Stone magazine (Random House, 1992). A serious illustrated guide to rock history with lots of photos.

Yes Yes Y'All: The Experience Music Project Oral History of Hip-Hop's First Decade by Jim Fricke and Charlie Ahearn (Da Capo Press, 2002). Lavish photo/oral history of hip-hop's birth.

Punk Is Dead Punk Is Everything by Bryan Ray Turcotte and Doug Woods (Gingko Press, 2007). A study of punk culture filled with show flyers and photos from 1977 to the present.

The Art of Rock Posters from Presley to Punk by Paul Grushkin (Abbeville Press, 1999). Rock concert posters from every era.

Glam! An Eyewitness Account by Mick Rock (Vision On Publishing, 2006). Classic glam era photo book. Glitter, makeup, and lots of David Bowie.

---

it comes to shows. You don't ever have to play a single bar in your whole life if you don't want to. You can say no to whatever you aren't into. You can be the singer who builds her career by playing 190 shows a year on a houseboat that cruises up and down the Mississippi. Playing weird little non-venues, or the corner, or the food court at the mall doesn't have to be what you do because you're too young to play shows in a bar. It can be what you are doing because that's what you are choosing.

Most people love music, but they don't go to clubs and see bands play. They have to put their kids to bed, they have to do their homework, or they have to go to field hockey practice. They wind up listening to music on their iPods or to the radio in their cars. They see maybe two concerts a year, of their super favorite acts, and they pay $72.50 and it's a thirty-thousand-seat venue at the fairgrounds, and they are sitting eight hundred feet away and watching the show on a Jumbo-tron screen. They don't get to connect with music or musicians in the course of their normal lives. Playing someplace that isn't a club, playing for free, playing someplace that is all ages, playing a spot where people could just happen by—you are bringing the music to people. It's a real cool act of sharing. Even if you play at a busy train station during rush hour,

Blondie frontwoman Debbie Harry takes to the stage in the band's early days.

people will stop and listen. And even if they aren't super into your music, they are going to think about what you are doing because you're a real human performing a song (not an American Idol on TV or an MP3 in their playlist). What you are doing will reconnect them with music in some way.

For some, playing music is about getting the audience to like you or your songs. But there is another part to being a musician that doesn't have anything to do with a career or popularity—it's about putting something interesting into the world. Aldous Huxley once said, "After silence that which comes nearest to expressing the inexpressible is music." One of your duties as a musician is to express that inexpressible—the things that people can't say on their own, the perfect theme for their mood or feelings, the truth that no one is willing to speak.

Being an ambitious musician doesn't have to mean you are just doing whatever it takes for you to "make it." When you are thinking about putting together a show, think about what would be fun for the audience, not just what's going to make you look cool. Think about what sort of shows always happen and things bands never do. How can you change things up? How can you create a different type of show experience?

Playing in public spaces where all different people feel welcome and comfortable, where anyone, no matter how young they are can come and see you—that seems like no big deal, right? But it totally is! Most concerts are at bars, and are for people who are over twenty-

one. Some of those people don't even care that much about music; they just want to hang out. But you don't have to try to achieve in a system that excludes you/your band. You can make your own system, whatever you want it to be like. All ages. Girls only. Outdoors only. Free. Cheap. In the morning. Roving. Play a show today, in an hour. Or once a year on Arbor Day. There's no reason not to do it how you dream it and make it *really* special, every single time you do it.

GOING BOOK WILD

There are three ways to book (set up) a show for your band: through a promoter, through another band, and through the venue itself. The easiest way is through a band. Talk to your friends in bands, or talk to bands you go see, and tell them your band is looking to play some shows. If there is a band in your city that is also a newish/small band that you like but don't know, send them a message on MySpace and ask them if maybe they'd want to play a show together. You may have to network a little bit before someone sends you the e-mail that says, "Hey, wanna open our show at the Smell on May 11?" If a local headlining band is playing a show, they will ask one or two bands they like to open for them; the promoter or the club booker might add another band as well.

Saying "go network" or "make friends" is easier said than done, I know, but a huge part of being in a band is forming a community with other creative, like-minded people. When you go see bands, introduce yourself and say you have a band and that you think you'd be good on a bill with them. If you are nice and confident and ask for what you want, this can get you pretty far. Fortunately, I have always been in a band with a member who was really friendly, who could talk to anyone and befriended every band we played with. If someone in your band is a naturally social person, even if your band is terrible (many of mine were), you can still get shows.

BOOKING WITH PROMOTERS

Another way to book a show is to go through a promoter. A promoter is someone who doesn't work for one particular club or venue but who puts together a show and then finds the right space for it. That might be a bar, a music club, or nontraditional venues like an Elks Lodge or bowling alley. A promoter will usually arrange a local show for a touring band that is coming through town on tour, rather than arrange nightly shows for local bands.

There are a few ways to approach a promoter to get a show with them (that is, if you don't already know them). Look on the flyer for an upcoming show, and there should be a name—something like Mean Kitty Productions or Hands Up Houston Presents or Chi-Boogie Shows—that tells you who is putting on the show. There may be a website or phone number. If not, do a Google search of the presenter's name, or look on MySpace.

Your next step is to call, or if you are going to a show that they are presenting, ask a staff member at the venue if the

PEOPLE WHO BOOK SHOWS CAN BE A LITTLE MEAN

Promoters and club booking agents have a reputation for being impatient. All of them are frantically busy and every band in the city wants something from them. They have a million demos and e-mails to get to, 110 posters that need to go up before Thursday, and tickets to be sold. Be reasonable and to the point, and they shouldn't be *too* rude to you. If they are, don't take it personally. Promoters are just trying to do their jobs and are that way with everyone. Don't get discouraged by it.

promoter is there. Have a demo ready to give to the promoter. Initial contact and first impressions can make a big difference, in person is always best if you can swing it. Another option is contacting them via e-mail or MySpace. You don't have to make a big pitch, just tell them your name, and that your band is looking to play a show, and include a link to your MySpace page. Even better: If there is an upcoming concert with no opening band listed, and it's still a few weeks away, ask if they have booked an opening band for that show.

If the promoter seems really busy, standoffish, or short with you, ask if there is a better way to contact them. They may have a specific system they follow like, "Send me music and then call me two weeks after that." Lots of promoters and venues have pages on their websites that explain how and when to contact them. Go by whatever it says there (they'll appreciate that you've done your homework) and call a week or two later to follow up.

With a promoter, arrangements are (usually) less formal than with a club. They're individuals, not a company with a staff, and for most of them, putting on shows is not a full-time job, it's something they do because they like to. Don't expect to get the money deal worked out in advance. They probably won't know how much they can pay you until the show is over, but they might just offer you a flat $20 to $50 and tell you that load-in is at 5:30.

CLUB BOOKING

To book a show at a club, try calling in the late afternoon. Rock clubs don't keep banker's hours; they're on rock 'n' roll (RNR) time. In RNR time, the workday is about 3 P.M. to 3 A.M. After 3 or 4 P.M., call the club, ask to speak to the booker, and do the same little spiel—name, band name, looking to play a show. A lot of clubs have Mondays or another night reserved for new band night. Ask about this. When you talk to a booker, she'll tell you what to do next. It might be, "Send a demo and we'll call you." She might ask how many people you can bring in to the club or where else you've played. She *might* blow you off. But get an e-mail or mailing address—whatever it is you need to get them your music, and ask the best way or best

time to follow up. Do what she requests, and again, get in touch a week or two later whether she tells you to or not. Persistence pays off.

We're going to skip ahead to the hopeful conclusion, and past the part where the promoter never calls you back and you spend a lot of time with her voice mail. That's frequently the reality, which is why alternative locations (see pages 144–145) are so appealing. Lots of promoters and clubs aren't going to want to give you a show until you can draw fifty or so people to see you play. If you're

patient, open to whatever opportunities arise, and chill when people (promoters, clubs, people in charge of stuff) don't see the awesomeness potential of your band, it's going to save you some torment and energy—energy that can be used for writing new songs and perfecting your playing skills.

Many people are very sensitive about their bands and want absolutely everyone to like their music. They only want the big breaks and only value the opening slot for the cool out-of-town band, as if that's all that matters. You will meet these people along the way—who only want the big stuff, who only see a long route of perfect steps to take to a magic place where everyone loves their music. The reality is that, while they are busy agonizing over the future and the "right" way to get there, they are missing out on all the fun, dismal, weird, and exciting stuff that happens to their bands in the present. You can (and should!) have high hopes for your art, but every little step of the way is just as important as the first time you headline the Oakville Verizon Dome to fifty thousand

HUNTING YOUR HAUNT

Make sure you are booking at a venue that is appropriate to your band's sound. If you are a metal band, you want to steer clear of the jazz club or the honky-tonk bar by the airport. Scope out the venues where the small bands you like play regularly.

screaming people. Plus, everyone knows, once you get famous, it's all downhill from there.

OH YEAH, WHERE WERE WE?

You've gotten a date from the promoter, and, initially, they are going to pencil you in. Soon after, you will call (or they will) and confirm the show. You want to make sure they tell you specifically "It's confirmed" before you go make flyers and start inviting people. When they confirm, they should fill you in on the essentials.

★ Load-in time

★ How much you will be paid or if it's a percentage of what they make that night

★ Where you are on the bill

You will tell them:

★ Your technical needs, if any, and what your band setup is ("standard bass, drums, two guitars, and three singers")

You will ask:

★ Do we get a sound check?

★ Are you doing posters for the show?

★ Is this number the best way to reach you?

★ Do we get a guest list?

Even when dealing with a legit venue, sometimes all the info they'll give you is a load-in time and if you're getting a sound check. Once your band is bigger and mostly playing legit clubs *or* if you have a booking agent who sets up shows for you, your shows will be contracted. A contract for a show is a binding agreement that outlines what you will do for the club (show up, play) and what the club itself is responsible for (what they're paying you, drinks, guest list, and load-in and set times). It'll also have an "Act of God" clause, which means, basically, if a natural disaster (extreme weather, national emergency) occurs, they don't have to put on the show or pay you. It's unlikely that your shows will be contracted unless a) you are opening for a big band at a big venue, b) you are moderately popular and touring out of town, or c) you are drawing more than two hundred people in your hometown.

YOU HAVE A SHOW BOOKED: NOW WHAT?

This is one of my favorite parts: making the flyers. Even when the club or promoter says that they are doing posters, you must always do your own posters, too—and here's why:

1 Clubs and bookers *love love love* bands that promote their own shows. It makes their job easier; it'll make them want to have you back. Most bands are pretty lazy about this, and it'll make your band stand out. Drop some off to the club or send a couple over to the promoter, so they can hang them in the club.

2 They are putting on five shows a week, and they can't give yours the same special attention that you can.

A PICTURE'S WORTH A THOUSAND WORDS

When you design your flyer, use text, make drawings, take a photo, or get inspiration from sources around you. Just make sure the end result is readable and enticing. Here are some ideas to inspire your next flyer.

- ★ Any book with pictures
- ★ Textbooks
- ★ Old magazines
- ★ Newspapers
- ★ Old movie stills
- ★ Books about nature
- ★ Good pictures of your band playing live
- ★ Medical encyclopedias
- ★ Old cookbooks
- ★ Google image search
- ★ Specialty magazines (*Cat Fancy, Newsweek, Good Housekeeping*)
- ★ Instruction manuals

- ★ Supermarket circulars
- ★ Coloring books
- ★ Collections of clip art and graphic design

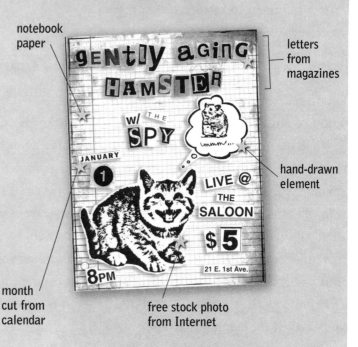

notebook paper

letters from magazines

hand-drawn element

month cut from calendar

free stock photo from Internet

3 The club may not be very good with promotions and flyers or they may not know how to reach fans of your band or style of music.

4 Making flyers is fun and is an expression of your band's style. It helps create an identity for your band.

The flyers you make are going to be in three forms: a little poster, handbills, and something to send around online. The posters are to hang on bulletin boards or drop off at the record store, or hang up wherever you see other show flyers. Get some tape and a staple gun (worth the investment) and hit up the coffee shops and the skate shop and wherever people who like music in your town hang out.

To make handbills (a little handout that could fit in someone's pocket), shrink the flyer down so that you can fit four of them on a page. Copy the page, then cut them apart, and pass those out to your friends or just people you run into that you know—like an invitation. Distribute twice as many as you think you need (if the venue where you're playing holds fifty people, hand out a

hundred handbills) and always keep a couple with you.

For online promotion, you can scan the flyer or make a different one on the computer that you can e-mail to your band's e-mail list, forward to your friends, and put up on MySpace or Facebook.

The flyer should have all the important information on it:

* Your band's name
* Where you are playing
* The address
* The date
* What time the show starts
* How much it costs
* What other bands are playing

Your flyer needs to be easy to read and understand, but it also has to look cool. Use images that'll communicate what sort of event it's going to be. If it's all Florida-style death metal, you aren't going to want to use a picture of frolicking puppies; you will want to use a picture of something evil-looking. If your band is retro, maybe you'd use an image from an old magazine. If your band is political, you might use a picture from the news

GO-GO'S

HONG KONG CAFE

JAN. 18-19

CONTROL YOURSELF

WITH *purge*

BARKMARKET.

and **L-7!**

subpop

PYRAMID 101 AVE A

TUESDAY SEPT 19 9:30

FA MI LY

GRAND OPENING PARTY

FREE

SUNDAY, FEB. 25. 7p
LAVENDER
DIAMOND
and NO AGE
and also THEM JEANS
and Artwork & Installation by
SAELEE or MATTHEW THURBER
436 N. FAIRFAX, 90036

45 GRAVE   9:00 pm

SCREWS   FEAR

STARWOOD   NOV. 11 TUES

Flyers should be clear, and include all
the crucial info about your show.

"Do it for yourself.
Don't do it because
it seems cool. And don't
do it to get confirmation.
It's hard because you
either have people who
like you because they
say you're hot or you
have people who hate you
because you're a girl. But
if you're doing it because
you love it and it's what
you love to do, then it's
not hard."

HALEY WILLIAMS, PARAMORE

or a famous picture of a demonstration. Think about what you are trying to get across. You want something that catches people's attention.

THE RULES

Don't use pictures of other bands. Don't use a picture of someone you know without his or her permission. Don't use a picture of someone you know personally and don't like (a defaced picture of a celebrity or political figure, fine, the girl you sit next to in biology, not). Don't use offensive or especially disturbing images (e.g., dead or dying people or animals, anything to do with genocide).

Whatever you go with, stick to one main image, rather than having several on the same page, but a cool-looking collage is always rad. If your band has a logo, use it. If you can make the flyer with more than one color on it, do it—it classes things up. The amount of effort you make in creating your flyer shows that your band is serious and fun.

MAKE A GOOD IMPRESSION

With promoters and club bookers, though they love music, what they do is a business. Anything you can do to make their job easier and any opportunity you have to make a good impression will mean more opportunities for your band. Basic manners are a good way to start: Be on time, don't play longer than you are supposed to, say thank you, be polite and professional. Believe me, they and the other people you are dealing with (sound people, lights, door person) will remember. Saying thank you and telling people you appreciate their help is really simple, but most musicians don't think to do that. Rock jobs are thankless jobs that don't pay very much, and people do them because they are passionate about music. Be gracious, responsible, and reasonable and you will gain allies and make lasting connections with people who can help you out.

Even when your band is totally amateur, be professional. This means playing like the room is packed full of people screaming your name even if there are only sixteen people there. Pouting and acting like you are too cool won't win anyone over. Don't just act like you are into it—BE into it—no matter if the only people watching are the drummer's stepdad and the sound person. You don't need to be doing flying kicks or anything, just show that what you are doing matters to you.

PROMOTION

Promoting your band can sometimes feel awkward because it's like being a saleslady for your own work. There are lots of effective ways to promote your work without being cheesy or pushy.

Inviting your friends to your shows can be hard, and the last thing you want is to feel like people are coming out of obligation. Plus, playing to your friends is sometimes the most difficult because you actually care what they think. Part of being friends is supporting each other— you go to your friends' basketball games, so let them show up and cheer for you while you do your thing. Who knows, they may get

Nina Simone, "The High Priestess of Soul," began playing piano as a young girl.

inspired to start a band, too. E-mail invitations and little reminder notes to your friends if you can't bring yourself to do it in person.

PERSONAL CONNECTIONS

After you play a show, don't disappear backstage or go take a nap in your van. Hang out! Go sit behind the merch table, and the people who saw you play will come talk to you. Someone here in the Lions Club hall in Grand Rapids, Michigan, loved something that you came up with in your living room. And he wants to tell you about it—there is no more important place to be than there, making this person's acquaintance. You don't have to be instant best friends with people, just be genuine. In return, you get validation, a possible friendship, and certainly a fan.

Hanging out and being friendly builds community. It's not just about selling your T-shirts. If you are on tour and you wind up chatting with someone, the next time you come through Denver, you might have a place to stay, or that girl will bring her friends, or she might

BUTTONS AND PATCHES AND STICKERS, OH MY!

Once you connect with people who liked your show, don't let them forget it! Make some stickers, buttons, or patches with your band's name and give them away. Everyone loves free stuff.

set up a show so your bands can play together. Being nice to people and then staying in touch with them (e-mail list) will build you a grassroots fan base that all the large-scale promotions in the world (publicists, advertising) can never buy you.

If you are cool to people at the show, the next day they are going to tell their friends on the late shift at Orange Julius, "I met the bassist from Mini-Dog last night and she was super cool." One of her Orange Julius co-workers sees your flyer for your next show and calls her friend and says, "I hear this band is supposed to be cool; we should go." Magic. Now you have a fan base.

THE E-MAIL LIST

Every show you play, no matter what, have an e-mail list handy. Even if there is no merch table to sit behind, and you have to stand and hold the clipboard, looking like you are hawking a petition, you *must* have the e-mail list at every show. After each show, type the collected names and e-mail addresses into a Word file or your e-mail program, so that next time you are playing a show, you can contact fans who have already showed interest. You don't want to harass people, but whenever something is happening with your band (new songs on your MySpace, upcoming shows, new T-shirts) you want to tell them. This method is free and it works.

THE INTERNET

As soon as you are a band, make a MySpace profile, and a Facebook page, (or whatever networking site makes sense for you). If you are at all serious about your band, make your own separate website. While MySpace and Facebook are really useful, ultimately, you want to direct and drive people to your site. It's more personal, and you don't have to fit the MySpace or Facebook format. Plus, these networking sites won't be around forever. Something could happen and your page could get deleted. Suddenly, you have no idea how to reach those 4,223 "friends" you had accumulated. By driving people toward your own website, you can have something that is unique and personal, something that is an extension of your band and your vision; and most importantly, people can sign up for your e-mail list. You can manage that information on your own and you can get in touch with the people that like your band, regardless of whether they've abandoned their MySpace accounts.

Give your fans a reason to check your website by posting MP3s or remixes or having contests.

PRESS AND OTHER PROMOTION

Once you make a demo and/or start playing shows at venues, you can begin promoting your band to people who write about music. Start by contacting the places where you read about shows, as well as the websites and blogs where you find out about music. Are there specific sites that write about the kind of music you play? Is there a column in your newspaper that is just about local bands? Is there a weekly paper that previews concerts or reviews CDs? Is there a blog that posts MP3s of local bands? Is there a music site that all the kids in your school read? These are the places you want to start.

Track down the music writer or the entertainment editor (names should be listed on the site or in the masthead of

> "Sometimes I forget that I'm a musician [...] [Yesterday,] while I was doing the little sound check I thought, 'Oh yeah, I'm a musician.' When you're doing all this promotion and all the interviews you sometimes forget that the real point is that you play music."
>
> **LESLIE FEIST**

the publication) and e-mail him or her three or four weeks before your show to give the details (time, cost, location, other bands on the bill) and the link to your MySpace page/band website. A short note of introduction is good, with a little blurb about your band (e.g., "We're a pop-metal quintet from Boise and this is our demo release show"). Whenever your band has something important going on (you're recording a record, you signed to a label, you're

HIT THE BOOKS:

EVERYONE'S A CRITIC

Here are six powerful, must-read titles from another kind
of rock icon—the critic.

Beginning to See the Light: Sex, Hope, and Rock-and-Roll by Ellen Willis (Wesleyan University Press, 1992). Ellen Willis was the first and best known female rock critic, and she loved loved loved rock 'n' roll. Very real, smart, and feminist; she influenced everyone who came after.

Stranded: Rock and Roll for a Desert Island edited by Greil Marcus (Da Capo Press, 2007). Rock critics write about the one album they'd bring to a desert island. One of the classic books of music writing.

Psychotic Reactions and Carburetor Dung: The Work of a Legendary Critic: Rock 'n' Roll as Literature and Literature as Rock 'n' Roll by Lester Bangs, edited by Greil Marcus (Anchor, 1988). Lester Bangs' writing conveyed his love (and occasional hate) for music in a way that no one else ever did. He was funny, righteous, and passionate. This is one of my very favorite books.

Mystery Train: Images of America in Rock 'n' Roll by Greil Marcus (Plume, 2008). Elvis, Robert Johnson, Sly Stone, The Band, and Randy Newman and the American Spirit. Slightly nerdy, but one of the key books of rock criticism.

Rock She Wrote: Women Write about Rock, Pop, and Rap by Evelyn McDonnell (Cooper Square Press, 1999). An essential collection of work from all the great female music critics and writers.

Love Is a Mix Tape: Life and Loss, One Song at a Time by Rob Sheffield (Three Rivers Press, 2007). Music-geek boy meets rock-critic girl, they geek out together, a million mix tapes are exchanged, boy loses girl, music heals the wound.

going on tour, the dude from Radiohead wore your band's shirt on TV), let these writers and editors know.

Getting press helps you reach a wider audience, brings people to your shows and makes clubs want to have you back. If you book a show at a legit/semi-legit place, ask the promoter to e-mail you a media list. Most clubs have a list of places to contact to help promote the show. The list will have the contact info of press people, websites, and college radio stations. Call and/or e-mail those people a few weeks in advance with information and see if they can hook up a preview. They might not be able or interested in doing anything, but maybe they have space to run a photo, or maybe they want to come to the show. When you first e-mail them, there are a few things you should have on hand to offer them that'll make the most of your promo efforts:

★ A hi-resolution color photo of your band. It doesn't need to be fancy. A group shot where everyone looks half-cool and has their eyes open will do.
★ Songs on your MySpace

★ A bio (see below)
★ A download link to your demo or album
★ A downloadable press kit or links to any other press you've gotten
★ A link to your website if you have one

Here is an example of an e-mail you might send to a media person. It doesn't have to be exactly like this, but this should give you an idea of what info should be included:

Hi _____,

I'm Becky from The Mystical Rats. I wanted to give you a heads-up that we're opening for Judas Priest at the Oakland Coliseum on 9/14. Let me know if you are interested in writing about the show. We have a photo, press kit, and bio available and I can e-mail them to you. The new songs from our demo are up on our MySpace page at [insert link here]. If you are interested in coming to the show, I can put you on the guest list. It should be fun.
Talk to you soon.
Thanks,
Becky Smith

You can also provide the links to all your downloadable stuff at the bottom of the e-mail. People at newspapers and weeklies, especially, are really busy and may not get back to you. If you provide everything they would need to write about the show/record, it betters your chances considerably. You don't need to give them your band's life story or kiss up or beg—in fact, it's better if you don't. If you are only playing basements, parties, and garages—they probably can't write about those shows, but if you are doing something especially cool like playing the park/political rally/skate park/a fundraiser for your dog's appendectomy that might be enough to get them to write a story. If you're doing something unusual that would make for an interesting story, definitely drop them an e-mail.

PROMOTING YOUR BAND TO BLOGS

Promoting your band to blogs is just like promoting to regular press people, but the key is to provide links to an MP3 that you have up somewhere. If you don't have a website, you can upload your song(s) to a file-hosting site like Yousendit or Mediafire. For blogs that aren't in your city, you don't need to bother telling them about shows, unless you are touring. If you are touring, let them know, even if you aren't touring to their city, because most blogs have readers from all over the country. Even if they are in Montreal and you are doing a five-date run to Fresno and back, mention something like "We're touring next month, the dates are on our MySpace page," or include them at the bottom of the e-mail.

One thing that works to your advantage as a new band

is that music blogs are really into discovering and sharing unknown bands. People who do MP3 blogs loooove to write about bands that no one else has heard of. If you are a reader or a fan of that blog, mention that as well.

Remember to share what's new and interesting—whether it's a new demo or a new show, they'll want to know important stuff. And remember to include any relevant web links or tour dates. Here are your sample pitches:

Hey _____,

My band Egyptian Legwarmers just finished our demo and I wanted to send you the link to it. We recorded it ourselves in my grandma's attic. We're still really only playing parties around here in Pittsburgh, but we're going to try and tour to Columbus this summer. If you need more info, here's our website [insert link] and there is a bio up on our MySpace [insert link].

Thanks!
Becky

Hi _____,

I saw that you posted an old Melt Banana song the other day and thought you might like this new song that my band Gently Aging Hamster just recorded [insert link]. We're working on the songs for our first demo right now, and this is the first one we finished. We're playing in Montreal next month if you want to come check us out.

Thanks!
Becky
[MySpace link]
[Website link]
Tour dates:
4/15 Pittsburgh
4/16 New York
4/17 Montreal

You can also promote your shows/demo to the radio station at the college in your town, using the same method. You will want to contact the programming director, or, if there is a radio show on there that you listen to, contact the DJ. The same thing goes for podcasts. It's just a matter of hunting people down on the Internet and focusing attention on your fine, fine band.

WRITE A BIO

A bio is the story of your band. It's mostly to help writers or other people who are interested in your band to find out what you are about. If you are a new, young band that has just started playing shows and none of your members also happen to be in Pearl Jam, you probably don't have that much of a story to tell. Your story is that you have formed a band and that you are not famous, which is not a unique story. Fortunately, you do have two things that make you stand out from ninety-six percent of the other bands on the planet: You are young and you are female.

People who work with music, especially the people who write about it, are always looking for an interesting angle for a story. Most of the bands, since the dawn of rock 'n' roll, are comprised of four twenty-seven-year-old dudes who don't have much of interest to say, and their music sounds like either Metallica or The Rolling Stones. Writers are generally excited by new bands, young bands, and bands with girls in them. You are all three—and make for an interesting story.

Band bios should have the basic history of the band and describe what you sound like and whatever is interesting about your band. If you have an unusual gimmick—for example, you wear bear

costumes, have a laser light show, have fourteen members, or all your songs are about Abe Lincoln—include that information and a few sentences about what inspired you to do that. If you have released an album, toured, or played with anyone famous or half-famous, that is important to mention. If you're part of a scene that is exploding with creativity, or the only speed-polka band in town, these are good angles. Use anything that'll set you apart from the rest.

Things you want to avoid in your bio:

★ Being over-the-top. Extreme hype or exaggeration is unnecessary.

★ Comparing yourselves to too many bands or listing *all* of your influences.

★ Comparing yourselves to bands that a lot of bands sound like (e.g., The Beatles, Rolling Stones, Fall Out Boy) *or* comparing yourself to totally unknown bands.

★ Making unflattering comparisons to animals ("like a cross between Bjork, the Smiths, and a cat in a blender"). Actually, avoid all comparisons to animals.

★ Writing an epic. Half a page, or three hundred words, is plenty.

★ Endless unimportant details about changes in the lineup. ("After the second practice, Bobby's cousin Don Quixote joined the band on keyboards but quit after six months and was replaced by Carla, who Jenny knew from horse camp . . .")

★ Mentioning that you are ex-members of bands that no one will have ever heard of. If you were previously in a band that played a lot of shows and/or made records that someone in your city might know about, that's okay to mention.

★ Being vague or being too technical

★ Insulting other bands, popular trends, or rock critics

★ Outright lies

★ Swearing

★ Saying you are going to take over the world (even if you intend to).

Write the bio like you are writing a short article about your band. It should be in the third person, have proper grammar and punctuation, and include the five Ws (who, what, when, where, why). Maybe include a quote or two (you can interview your bandmates) that represents what you are—smart/ambitious/creative—etc. It can be hard to write about yourself, so if you have a friend who is a good writer, ask her to help you write or write it for you.

Some questions to think about before you begin your bio:

* Is there anything interesting or unusual about how you formed/met each other?

* What is special or different about your band?

* What do other people like about your band?

* How would you summarize your musical vision in seventy-five words or less?

Here are two different approaches to the band bio. In the examples, note that one (below) is more streamlined, factual, and to the point; the other (next page) reads more like an article.

THE PURELY INFORMATIONAL BIO

This bio is just the no-frills facts, no opinions or selling points.

The Mesmerizing 5 began playing together as a trio in Minneapolis in May 2008, and quickly expanded to a quartet with Becky Stark (vocals), Chad Clark (bass), Mike Taylor (guitar/organ), and former Pearl Jam guitarist Mike McCready on drums. They released their first EP, *Shadows & Light: A Tribute to Joni Mitchell* in April 2009 on Epic Records. After the release of the record, the band toured throughout Japan and Canada opening for Earth, Wind & Fire. After returning to the U.S., they went back into the studio with noted producer J. Robbins to record their debut full-length *In Yo Face, Klaus Nomi!* The album is a departure from the band's previous work and was influenced by traditional Indian raga and the classic hard-core beats of Gorilla Biscuits. The band will be touring the U.S. through the summer.

THE MINI-ARTICLE BIO

This type of bio highlights what the story and ideas behind your band are.

Becky Stark and Becky Smith began MegaFence as a way to try out new musical ideas and quickly turned into Minneapolis's best undiscovered band. Word of mouth has since spread their vibrant, danceable, political songs and their live shows routinely draw a hundred people into packed basements all over town.

"I had never sung before MegaFence, but had always dreamed of having a band," says Stark. "Becky lives down the block from me and whenever I would go over to her house, she would play me songs she was working on. One day she played me 'Rainbow Mist' and I was really inspired. I went home and wrote down some lyrics and the next day I came back and said 'I have an idea.' And that was in October of 2004 and we've been playing together ever since."

Though MegaFence is only a duo, they have a huge sound. Employing the use of three Marshall stack amps and a specially tuned harpsichord, Smith creates an impenetrable, sparkly wall of melody. Despite her use of an old-fashioned instrument, Smith finds her inspiration in modern sounds. "My biggest influences are industrial noises—the buses going by my house, loud machinery, and construction. I try to replicate their rhythms in my playing," says Smith.

Since their formation, MegaFence has recorded two demos and a new EP. The EP features an eleven-minute instrumental "Do They Know It's Christmas?" that is a staple of their live shows, and will be released later this year on cassette.

The key is (if you're not going for the purely informational bio) to make your bio what you want other people to say about you, because some writers will just reword your bio when they write about you. It's not unusual at all, actually. Don't go too bananas and call yourself the biggest genius talent ever to come outta Illinois since Miles Davis. Nope. It's more like, if you want people to notice the influence of '60s garage rock in your songs, or that your songs have a pro-girl theme, you should point it out. If your band is part of an obscure genre—say you are California-style black metal or anarchist crust punk—and you want to be known that way—express that in the bio (otherwise, they might just call your band "weirdo metal"). Never assume that the "music professional" that's listening to your demo has any idea what your music is about.

CHAPTER 5

TURN IT UP

Here's the reality: Your band may never make more than $50 for playing a show. If you are starting your band with the idea that there might be a little pot of gold at the end of the band practice rainbow, here's another thought to add into the fantasy: It costs you money to be in a band. Being in a band never stops costing money. You have to pay for equipment you need, maybe a practice space, gas to shows, snacks, picks, new drumheads every once in a while. If you aren't playing clubs, or shows where you make more than $20, and want a little cash to help with whatever expenses you have, play a party. Convince a popular friend to have a party, charge $5 to get in, and even if you only have eighteen people there, that's still something. Do that a few times and you will have money to buy a P.A. for your practice space.

MIND YOUR OWN (BAND) BUSINESS

Costs can add up fast, but there are ways to limit your expenses and keep your band excited about playing. Here are some tips for keeping it cheap:

- Find a place to practice for free.
- Keep your expenses low by recording your demo on your computer, and borrowing the things you need (mics, pedals), rather than buying them.
- A smaller lineup. The fewer members a band has, the cheaper everything is.
- Exist only on the Internet. You don't need gas money, a van, or T-shirts when you are online-only.

ONCE YOU MAKE A BUCK OR SEVEN

Get receipts so you can keep tabs on anything you spend band money on. Get a little binder to organize your stuff and keep track of your band funds, so that you know how much you've made or how much you need to come up with to cover band expenses. Expenses should be split evenly between every member of the band; one person should not have to put up more money than others. It's important to keep things as fair and democratic as possible. A creative situation that involves money, friendship, and art is an easy recipe for disagreements.

One person in your band—the same person who is updating the binder and playing accountant—should be in charge of getting paid after a show. Being consistent about this is important, because then everyone in your band knows who has the money and the booker/promoter will always know the right person to deal with.

If your band starts making money with shows and/or selling merch, you should pool any money you earn into a band fund. The band fund is for band expenses. This is money you should save, rather than divide up. Try to keep a savings reserve equal to three months' worth of your practice space rent or $150. Try to maintain that amount, so in case something happens or you don't play shows for a while, you still have things covered. Band money should only be used for band-related expenses and things that benefit the entire band. Some appropriate uses of band money include:

★ Practice space rental costs
★ Making/copying flyers

* T-shirts or other merch expenses
* Recording costs
* Gas to shows
* Special equipment for your stage show (e.g., lights, smoke machine, costumes)
* A lawyer
* P.A. for practice space
* A van/band vehicle
* The occasional pizza for band meetings, snacks, or a post-show meal if you made some cash. (Not all the time, but it's good for band morale.)
* AAA coverage for the band vehicle
* Insurance for the band vehicle
* Insurance for your equipment

"You have to kick doors open yourself. When people come up to me and say, 'Patti, nobody wants to hear my CD and I don't have enough money for equipment,' I say, 'Well, get a job, y'know?' That's what I did."

PATTI SMITH

* One person's equipment, unless the whole band agrees to it
* Individual lessons
* Presents for people
* Outfits for your cat
* Drugs

You won't necessarily have to spend money on all these things (hey, if your parents are still driving you to gigs because you don't have your license yet, sweet!—that's another cost you don't have to worry about), but the list is just meant as a guideline for things that might come up and are acceptable. On the flip side, there are definitely some things that band money should *not* be spent on:

Money problems can split up a band. The person in charge of the band's money should be open and communicative with everyone about what is happening with the money, so no one is in the dark. Also: The person who parked the van in the wrong place should pay the parking ticket, not the band.

DUTY NOW FOR THE FUTURE

It's a good idea to have one person be the main contact/communicator/business person for your band. Things like that tend to work out pretty naturally in a group. One person who is good with money and organized and friendly is ideal to be the in-band manager. The other people can be in charge of other stuff like making the flyers, driving/packing the van, or making or selling merch. Splitting duties is super important, and not just because it's the fair thing. When everyone in the band has a responsibility, it means everyone is trusted and trustworthy. It makes everyone feel important and included, and your band will be more like a family than a business. I was in a band once where, despite being a good driver and knowing how to count, I never got to drive the van or do merch. It made me feel like I was tagging along instead of being an actual member of the band. Duty, trust, and responsibility will help keep your band together.

WORKING WITH OTHERS

The more organized your band is about the business side of things, and the more you do things for yourselves, the more people will be interested in working with you. If you can make things happen on your own—booking agents, managers, labels—people will want to be involved in helping you. It's best to handle your business for as long as you possibly can before you start getting people outside the band to do it for you. Learning how to handle the reins before you turn them over to someone else sets you up to be

"I've been called quite a few things that weren't endearing because of my decision to follow my heart and follow the music that I feel passionate about. But I don't see those walls or limitations when it comes to music."

NONA HENDRYX, LABELLE

able to make better deals and smart, informed decisions about your career.

There are booking agents and managers who make a living by handling a hundred tiny bands. Try to avoid working with people like this. It's better to have no agent at all than work with someone who has too many bands to keep track of. You want to work with someone who has time to give your band special attention, especially because most managers take ten to fifteen percent of the money your band earns and booking agents take ten to fifteen percent of whatever you make on shows.

Hold out on hiring someone until you are a "bigger" band and are making decent money from shows or other band business. The more popular your band is by the time you get a manager, the more power you'll have to bargain with them, and the better your chances are of finding someone who only works with a couple of bands.

Whatever you do, don't hire a manager just to have one. Hire a manager when:

★ It's beyond your ability to handle all the business your band is doing because there is so much of it.

Lily Allen started taking singing lessons when she was eleven. Ten years later, her song "Smile" hit No. 1 on the U.K. charts.

★ If your band is doing really well and you are touring for months at a time and can't take care of things because you are away so often.

★ You are getting offered record deals from multiple labels.

★ Your band is popular and making money and you want some help steering your career for the long term.

Managers are good for administrative things; they are somewhere between a parent and a secretary. They take care of scheduling and coordinating appearances; they deal with all the people your band might work with

Cat Power (aka Chan Marshall) manages her own career.

(publicist, recording label, booking agent); they keep your website up to date, book your flights, and help you to achieve some of your bigger goals. One of the things managers can also help you do is try to make money on the publishing and licensing of your songs.

PUBLISHING

In terms of business, every song has two parts to it—the master, which is the recording of the song itself and the publishing, which is the words and the music. When you sign a record label contract, you are (usually) doing a deal to sell the master recording. Publishing companies do deals with the songwriter for the rights to the music and lyrics.

Every time a copy of a new record or an individual song is sold, the songwriter gets paid a mechanical royalty (a small fee) for each song. This is paid on every song that is sold so that the songwriter gets money whether an album is a success or not. This is a federal law that was created to protect songwriters, so they can make some money whether their record labels pay them or not. As of the release of this book, the mechanical royalty rate is 9.1 cents per song.

GETTING AFFILIATED WITH A PUBLISHER

Each member of your band who is involved with songwriting needs to become affiliated with a publisher. Publishers track what songs get played everywhere that music is played/performed (radio, TV, airplanes, Internet radio, etc.), and collect and distribute the money to the songwriters. They keep a percentage of the money as their fee. There are three companies—BMI, ASCAP, and SESAC. Anyone can affiliate with BMI and ASCAP (you fill out forms, basically), but for SESAC, you have to be invited. BMI and SESAC are free; ASCAP costs $10 per year. You can request info or apply online (ASCAP.com, BMI.com, SESAC.com).

With most publishing deals, the publisher will pay you money up front (called an advance), which has to be recouped. Recouping is like a debt you have with them; the company wants to make back the money they've paid to you. They get that back through mechanical royalties and any money your songs earn from being used in movies, TV shows, video games, commercials (called "synchs")—all of which pay a fee to use your song. Once your songs have earned back the "advance" money paid to you, all the money after that is split between you and the publisher.

There are also much more basic types of publishing deals where you don't get an advance. You affiliate with a publishing company who collects your mechanicals, and passes any money your songs make from synchs directly to you, keeping a little percentage of whatever you earn.

LEGALESE

Getting a record deal is a goal for most musicians. Having a label offer to put out your record is exciting; it means that someone is going to get behind your music and put it into the world for other people to hear. A record

"I've always had an attitude about managers. Unless they're really needed, they just confuse matters. They obviously have their own impressions of a direction and an image that is theirs, and surely it should come from within the actual structure rather than from outside. I often think that generally they're more of a hindrance than a help."

KATE BUSH ON WHY SHE WAS SELF-MANAGING HER CAREER AT AGE NINETEEN

Kate Bush was the first woman to top the UK charts with a self-written song.

deal (even if it's with your friend's teeny-tiny label) is a business transaction. Any time you are doing business that involves your music, you need to protect yourself and make sure that you aren't getting into something that is unfair to you. Whenever you are entering into a business relationship that involves your band or music, you want to be official and legal. It's *mandatory* that you get a music attorney who can help you navigate this stuff.

Most music-business deals go like this: A label or publisher gives you some money, and in exchange, you give them the legal rights to sell your music—the recordings, or the songs. Your music, because you created it, is technically your property. When you do deals, you are trading that property for cash and royalties and/or some kind of service; they then own what you made. They may own it for a certain period of time, or they may own it for all of eternity. The deal may give them the right to do whatever they want with what you have sold them, and/or it might give them the right to some of the money your music makes.

It's very important that you get a music attorney who understands and knows all parts of your deal. You want someone who knows the music industry and is familiar with what is a fair offer for the type of deal you are making, whether it's with a record, publishing, management, or sponsorship deal. You want someone who knows the stature of the label, your band, and the level of the deal. Don't use your mom's friend who is a tax attorney or does criminal law to look over your contract. If you don't know an entertainment lawyer who deals with new or young bands, ask around. Ask other bands or the booker at the club you regularly play at, or someone else in your area who works with music. If you use a non-music attorney who doesn't know the ins and outs of the music world, you can wind up in deals that don't benefit you.

Here's what you want to look for in an attorney: someone who is going to care about you even though you are a small band or doing a small deal. Find a lawyer who is used to working with new and unestablished bands; he or she should be someone who is not going to break you with bills, and someone you can easily get on the phone when you have questions.

Legal work can get expensive really fast. You want to find someone you can afford—you don't want to (and shouldn't) spend all the money from your record deal paying your lawyer. When you find an attorney you want to work with, ask them what their fee structure is and how they bill. Some bill for their hours, and others take a percentage of the money you get from your record deal. You can also ask for a retainer agreement with them, which states how long they'll work for you, what they're going to do, and what they're going to charge you.

You *absolutely* need to care about what every deal means long term, not just how much you'll be paid. Money is important, but so are your rights as an artist. You have to be concerned about both. Never, ever, *ever*, EVER sign anything you don't understand completely.

RECORD DEAL OR NO DEAL?

In the last few years a type of record deal called a "360 deal" has become a lot more common. A 360 deal is where you turn over most or all rights to your music: your merchandising (T-shirts, hoodies, posters, etc.), publishing, and the money you make from playing shows. In exchange, they will give you money up front—an advance—on what they think you might normally earn from all those things. This is called a multi-rights deal.

The first contract (or deal memo) that you get from a record label is not what you are going to sign. All contracts end up getting negotiated. The record label expects this. The first contract they send over may have everything written in their favor. The artist and their attorney are expected to come back with changes and then you wind up meeting in the middle somewhere. The first offer you get can always be improved on, so never settle for the first thing you see. Don't feel pressured. You do not have to take exactly what they are offering. If a record label is serious enough about their interest in you—remember, *they* want to sign you—then they aren't going to present it as a take-it-or-leave-it situation. It's never all or nothing.

STAY OUT OF TROUBLE: DON'T RIP OFF OTHER BANDS' SONGS

It's perfectly legal (and fun) to cover another band's songs; it is illegal to rip off another band's original song and call it your own. There are some famous bands that have been sued by other musicians for releasing songs that copied (or were too close to) theirs. (Little Richard sued Creedence Clearwater Revival, Wire sued Elastica, The Rubinoos sued Avril Lavigne—and they all won.) Sometimes it's a fine line between paying tribute to your influences and ripping them off. If your song is similar enough in the music and/or lyrics that it can be confused for another band's work, and your song becomes popular, the other band might come after you for some of the money you are making from it. With art it's hard to prove copyright infringement, but just to be safe, don't bogart other people's riffs and call them your own.

PRODUCER AGREEMENTS

Let's say you got a record deal, and it's time to go into the studio and make a record with a producer. You need to have

It will also explain what services the producer is going to provide, how much advance notice they need if your band is going to cancel a session, and maybe how many songs you are going to record.

"IN PERPETUITY" AND "RECOUPABLE"

The term "in perpetuity" is the most serious term you will encounter in a contract. It usually applies in the record company's favor: In exchange for a certain amount of money, they own what you have made, and they own it forever, subject to paying you royalties. Here's a quick guide to some terms that you should watch for as there is a long, long history of musicians and bands being in bad situations with their recording careers because they didn't totally understand what these terms mean.

"In perpetuity" means at least forever and nothing short of eternity. It usually applies to the ownership of master recordings, songs, videos, or other things the artist/band has made. If a record label owns your master recordings in

Before she was a platinum-selling rock goddess, PJ Harvey was an avid teenage saxophonist.

an agreement with the producer—they very well may provide you with one, but if they don't, you need to have one drawn up. It should say something about how much you will pay per hour, for how many days, and how soon after you finish you have to pay your bill (it's usually between thirty and ninety days).

perpetuity, it means that they own your record. Period. They get to decide what happens with it now and in the future.

"*Recoupable*" means an expense that the artist/band pays for out of their share of profits. The artist's share of profits is called royalties. In the recording and manufacture of an album, there are things the label pays for one hundred percent, and those are called non-recoupable. If something is recoupable, it doesn't mean that the artist has to write a check for her own money; the money is deducted against any profit from the sales of the record. They have to make that money back before you get any of your money.

ACCESSORIZING YOUR BAND

One of the best parts of being in a band is making all the stuff—the things that represent your band visually. Before you play a show or head out on tour, think about what items might be right for your band to make. T-shirts, hoodies, stickers, and buttons are the standard—they each give your fans something to take home and also turn

them into walking billboards (good for getting the word out). You can make whatever you want to. You could make tote bags, pillowcases, commemorative lunchboxes, masks of band members, a handcrafted lyric book—if you can make it, you can probably sell it.

MAKE SHIRTS, NOT MISTAKES

Don't blow your money on T-shirts until you are *positive* you can sell them. You don't need to go lay out $400 for 150 brand new T-shirts if you have only been playing shows for a few months, or if you are the opening band on a small regional tour. If you are going on a six-month tour opening for Nick Cave or Stevie Nicks, yes, by all means get some shirts. Until you have the fan base to merit expanding your line of merch, stick with selling little stuff—stickers and pins (see page 192), and your music.

If you are going to do shirts, do them cheap, and do them in batches of twenty to thirty at a time. The last band I was in, our guitarist designed and had printed up some of the ugliest T-shirts you have ever seen in your life (sorry, Dave). They looked like they were for a company picnic, not a rock band, and on top of that, he made a ton of them and they were kind of expensive. I don't think my bandmate was particularly serious when he suggested that if I didn't like them, make my own. But I did. I made a dozen bootleg T-shirts and sold them for $5 each. I used blank thrift-store shirts and printed them in my kitchen the day before the show using a Print Gocco. They weren't amazing, but I sold all of them at one show—people liked the one-of-a-kind nature of them. My bandmate's shirts? Still in boxes somewhere. The only person I have ever seen wearing one is my dad, and he got it for free. The moral of this story: Don't waste your money on accessorizing unless you know people will want the product.

MAKING BUTTONS

Buttons are the perfect giveaway because they are really cheap and easy to make. You can get a button maker and supplies for a few hundred buttons for about $80 total. They are cooler than stickers, they last for years, and you only have to make as many as you need.

If you want to make a whole, whole lot of buttons, I suggest ordering them from Busy Beaver Button Co. in Chicago. It's a woman-owned company that makes buttons for thousands of bands. If you have a band button, they probably made it. Check out prices and info online at www.busybeaver.net.

HOW TO STENCIL

I like to use a cardboard stencil or two and some cans of spray paint for making tees, tanks, and sweatshirts. It's simple, rad, cheap, *and* you can use your stencils over and over (and replicate them easily).

WHAT YOU WILL NEED:

- ★ Pen or pencil
- ★ X-Acto knife
- ★ Two 12 x 12-inch pieces of cardboard (three if you are doing a two-color shirt)

- ★ 1 to 2 can(s) of spray paint
- ★ Several pieces of newspaper

1 Mark your band logo or name (or whatever you want) onto one of the pieces of cardboard and then use the X-Acto knife to carve along the marked lines to create a stencil.

2 Slip the other cardboard piece between the layers of the shirt underneath where you want to put your design.

3 Place the cardboard stencil over the T-shirt where you want it to appear on the shirt.

4 Put it on the ground, on top of some newspapers.

5 Make sure the shirt is flat and that the stencil is sitting flat on it.

6 Shake up your spray paint and from a distance of about eight to twelve inches, spray it over the area so that the stencil gets filled in. You don't want to spray it super close because then it will bleed and soak the shirt and be blobby looking.

7 Remove stencil carefully and repeat the process on the remaining T-shirts. Optional: Wait until the first color is dry before adding a second color or design.

VARIATIONS

If you can't get your hands on spray paint, you can also stencil using a piece of vellum (it costs about a dollar at the art supply store), fabric paint, and a paintbrush.

If you want to be a little more pro, or be able to replicate an exact design many times, you can learn to silk screen your designs. This is a more involved process that is messy, fun, and requires space to lay things out to dry. You will also need transparencies, rubber gloves, a 250-watt photo bulb, photo emulsion, and some other chemicals. Once you do two or three silk screen projects you will be an old pro and you'll be creating special posters for your big shows, limited-edition shirts for your band, and album covers like it ain't no thing.

MAKING STICKERS

Stickers are another cheap and easy option for band merch. You can print out an 8 x 11-inch sheet of black and white designs, take them down to the copy store near you and have them copied on sticker paper. You'll probably have to cut them to size yourself. If you are into silk screening, you can get some sticker paper or vinyl sheets and do it yourself. If you want multicolor stickers or vinyl stickers, you'll have to have those manufactured—there are plenty of resources online. Diesel Fuel in Portland (dieselfuelprints.com) and Sticker Guy in Reno (stickerguy.com) are both good, reputable companies that a lot of smaller bands use.

TOURING

Touring is a way to build a fan base outside of your city and also a strange/great way to see the world. You may not get to tour the whole world, you might just get to the five neighboring states around Iowa, but it is an adventure nonetheless. Make a point to go on tour at least once in your life—it's one of the best parts of being in a band. You make friends, you come home with funny stories, and you get closer with your bandmates. It's like camp but louder. You also deepen your connection to the music community you are part of. Then there are the other perks that you don't get at home: sleeping on floors, eating rest-stop food, and strong arm muscles from moving equipment.

The best part of all is that you get to have a little vacation (I use that term lightly) from your regular life and your entire day revolves around playing your music. Even if you're only doing a three-day tour of upstate New York, you're a full-time musician for those three days. It doesn't matter if back home you're a misunderstood sophomore; tonight, here in this basement in Syracuse, you're whoever you want to be. When you're on the road, you're absolutely free, and all that really matters is what happens when you play your songs.

To start touring, first you have to build up what you have locally. You expand out, regionally, going farther and farther out and away from your city.

The author onstage on tour with the band Challenger.

Eventually you go from doing a week in the Midwest to two weeks on the East Coast, then to Canada, and then the rest of the world from there.

Here's the process, which begins with one fundamental question.

CAN YOU GO ON TOUR?

If you are under eighteen, there is at least one adult in charge of your life. Is he or she cool with you going on tour? Can your parents help make it happen somehow? Would they be open to driving your band on a four-date tour during your spring break? Is there an older sibling of someone in your band with a car or van and a lot of spare time? Perhaps a sister who is college-age, trustworthy, totally into your band, and doesn't have a job this summer? Going on tour is an uphill challenge if you aren't old enough to drive and/or travel by yourself, but there are ways you can make it happen.

CAN EVERYONE IN THE BAND GO? IF YES, WHEN?

Can everyone get permission and time off from their school (or jobs), if needed? Does everyone have spring break or the summer free? Plot out your schedules, discuss, beg parents, reconvene. Word of warning: Don't go during break if you have finals or important tests when you get home. Don't drag all your homework with you, thinking that you'll have time in the van and before sound check to study—you won't. When you are in the van, all you do is sing along with the stereo, write postcards, gossip, make gross jokes, and stare at what's going by. Everyone I know always drags some heavy book with them on tour, but nobody ever finishes *War and Peace* because you're all too busy going, "Was that a dog on the side of the road? That was big enough to be a wolf. I think it was a wolf." And then spending the following half hour talking about the grossest dead thing you've ever seen.

On tour, you spend a lot of time waiting and riding around, so there is downtime, but don't put too many expectations on yourself in terms of productivity—being on tour is just about being on tour.

DOES EVERYONE WANT TO GO?

Hopefully, you had that convo back when you put the band together about your goals. Everyone's got to be on board with the same plan. Touring is not something you want to be talking people into, because, despite being super-super-super fun, it's a lot of work with standing around and waiting mixed in. If someone is at all reluctant about venturing away from home in order to play for twelve people in Cleveland, actually doing it may not be the thing that changes her mind. You have to be pretty deeply committed to playing music in order to tour. Touring is not for casual enthusiasts or the faint of heart.

HOW LONG AND WHERE TO?

How long you can (or want to) be gone is going to determine how far from home you can get. You want to start by doing weekends and short trips. Just because you have the entire summer open does not mean you want to book a seventy-five-date tour that takes you from Portland to Puerto Rico and back. If you have five days free, you probably want to do a little loop that takes you no more than five hundred miles away. For the purpose of our example, let's say you and I have a band, Conflict Resolution, based in Chicago. A good loop is one that would go to some bigger cities and one or two smaller ones. We don't want to try to get to Vancouver and back in a weekend—unless we're getting paid $4,000 to open for Bjork, in which case we are flying.

Make tour posters and send them to show promoters in advance.

WHY ARE YOU GOING WHERE YOU'RE GOING?

Where you decide to go on tour should be based on some information or connection you have with some place or another band, promoter, or friend. Maybe you have just heard that a certain club is supposed to be really cool, or that your friend just played an amazing house show in Pittsburgh and seventy-five people showed up and there were free donuts.

MAKING YOUR CONNECTIONS WORK FOR YOU

Minneapolis is just over four hundred miles away from Chicago. We (our band, Conflict Resolution) played with the Minneapolis-based MegaFence (the awesome imaginary band in the promotions chapter) at a party a few months ago, and the singer Becky was super cool. We hit her up on MySpace to see if they could hook us up with a show, or set something up some time in the middle or end of July, which is a little over two months away. Maybe they are interested in also doing another date or two over that weekend?

Milwaukee and Madison are both a few hours away. Maybe they can't do Minneapolis because they already have a show booked the next week, but they can do a show in Mankato, about ninety minutes away, where they have some friends who put on shows at the skate park. And maybe they can also give us the info of the cool place in Minneapolis where they like to play and/or suggest good local bands to play with.

MILKING THOSE CONNECTIONS BY MAKING MORE

When you are calling around trying to put a tour together, you might reach dead ends or people who can't help you with a show on the day you need. Ask them if they can suggest someone else to try. You never want to come out of a conversation empty handed. If someone books shows, they know all the other people in town who do shows, and probably people in the next town. Just ask. You might have to call four peoples' friend-of-a-friend, and even if none of them are helpful for the Saturday night in Madison you need right now, you have phone numbers and e-mails for your next tour.

THE ACTUAL BOOKING PART

Let's look at a map. If we're going to go to Minneapolis, Milwaukee and Madison are on the way. Then we could do a smaller city an hour or two away (Mankato, St. Cloud—any place with a college) on the way back, and then someplace in Iowa (Des Moines, Cedar Rapids). If you have no contacts, friends, or friends-of-friends in Iowa, try sleuthing around on MySpace

YOUR TOUR

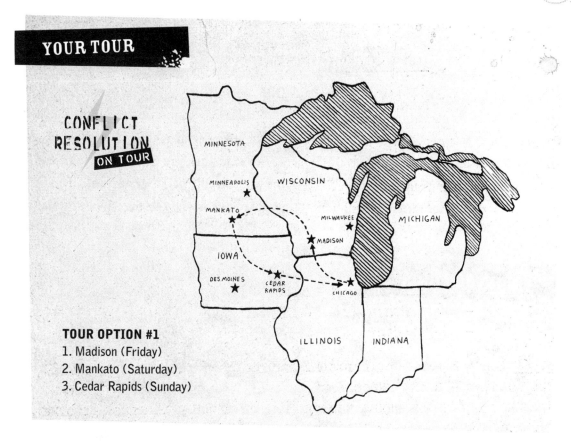

CONFLICT
RESOLUTION
ON TOUR

TOUR OPTION #1
1. Madison (Friday)
2. Mankato (Saturday)
3. Cedar Rapids (Sunday)

or Google up some clues. It's as easy as typing in "punk show Cedar Rapids"— you get the website of the main club and independent rock promoter there. It'll pull up current blogs about what shows are happening where, and you can deduce and track people down there. If Minneapolis falls through at the last minute, you still have a solid route (see map, above).

NAILING DOWN A DATE

Just like when you book a local show with a promoter, you have to be flexible and work with what dates they have available. What usually happens is you check with people and say you are looking for a show on one of these two certain days. Maybe they don't have any spots open then, but they have an opening two days later, which falls on the day you were headed back home. Instead of playing Madison before Minneapolis, now maybe you'll play on your way back and go to Iowa first. Or maybe you will just play Milwaukee on the way up and Madison on the way back and skip Iowa (see map, below). Does this sound like a scheduling nightmare? It is. Booking is a matter of shuffling around,

and a lot of maybes. Get the first show confirmed, and build the tour around it.

CONFIRMING

Confirming an out-of-town show works the same way as an in-town show (see page 157). Remember, you always want to hear the word "confirmed," because until then it's just a big maybe. Get the address for the

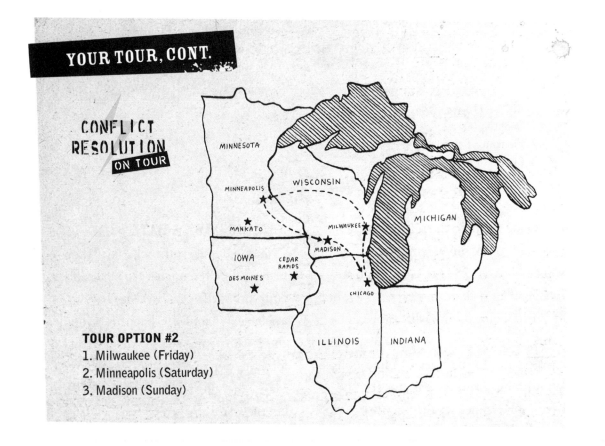

YOUR TOUR, CONT.

CONFLICT RESOLUTION ON TOUR

TOUR OPTION #2
1. Milwaukee (Friday)
2. Minneapolis (Saturday)
3. Madison (Sunday)

BOOK IN ADVANCE

If you are booking your tour shows with clubs and promoters, you need to book two to three months in advance. When you call about dates you are available (say a Sunday or Monday), and if the booker hears your music and is into it and wants to put you on the show, they will give you a hold on a date. A hold is tentative; it's not a confirmed show. It's potential commitment to one of your available days. Usually, when you call a club, there'll already be one or two holds on the date from bigger touring bands. It's kind of like a waiting list. Whoever called first gets first hold; second band gets second hold, and so on. If the band with first hold confirms, then the date is theirs for the show. The bands with the second and third hold may become the openers on the show, or if the first hold band already has opening bands on the tour, then the second and third hold bands don't get a show.

Once you start firming up your surrounding shows, you check back and either take off your hold on the date if you are going to play somewhere else, or confirm. For young bands just starting out, you might not get a hold; you might just get a yes or no.

promoter—because you aren't there to put up flyers for the show, mail some posters/flyers for the promoter to put up.

EXPENDITURES

Going on tour costs money. Before you book a tour you have to figure out whether you can afford it. How much will it cost in gas (figure how many miles per gallon your tour vehicle gets)? Also, budget for a hotel room (if there are more than four people in your band, you may need two rooms), especially if you are playing cities where you don't know people you can stay with. Even if you know you're going to make money at the shows, your band still needs to save up some money in advance. Save more money than you ever think you'll need—and then save a little more.

WHAT TO BRING ON TOUR

The first time I went on tour, I overpacked. I packed like I was going on a tour that was going from the spring until winter and needed to be prepared for the beach *and* a snowstorm. By the fourth day, I was sick of lugging this huge bag in and out of the van and my bandmates were teasing me because I had brought two coats (and heels and legwarmers). By the second week, I

PROS GET SHOWS

If you are on tour with other bands, introduce yourself at the first show to everyone on the tour—the band members and the crew. Exchange phone numbers with their tour manager (if they have one) in case you get a flat tire and are going to miss sound check. You don't need to be buddies with everyone, but it shows consideration and professionalism. You never know which of these people will provide an opportunity later. If you are cool and easy to work with, people will remember you and want to help you out.

When you're the opening band, show up on time and be prepared. If you find you aren't needed for a sound check, don't just up and disappear—the other sound checks might run short and you might get time to do one.

A good formula for ensuring you arrive on time is to tack on an extra hour for each four hours it will take to get there (so, if it's eight hours away, give yourself ten hours to get there). You will inevitably hit traffic, have to stop for gas, and eat. Plus, if you wind up getting a little lost, you can still make your load-in on time. Always leave extra time if you are headed to pretty much anywhere on the East Coast, Atlanta, Chicago, San Francisco, Houston, and Southern California.

was giving away my clothes to friends we stayed with. You will find that on tour, you wear the same stuff over and over. Maybe you bring a cool stage outfit or three to alternate between, but otherwise, just go with the necessities. If you are going on a month-long tour, you only need to bring a week's worth of clothes. One of the great things about America is that there are laundromats everywhere. You can get to Cleveland early and hit the washing machines before sound check. This is *way* better than dragging your entire closet with you—remember, between your guitar case and your amp, you already have enough gear to haul, and those people in the front row won't know you've been wearing the same jeans for three days.

By the second and third tours, I had my bag down to a science. Two pairs of jeans, one skirt for when I was feeling fancy, shorts, one pair of shoes, flip-flops, bathing suit (you never know when the opportunity to swim will arise), six T-shirts, and a hoodie. At one point, it got cold so I bought a jacket at a thrift store. Also, bring a

> "I find the most interesting thing is that people don't think we see them. We'll have people come to ten shows in a row. But then if I'm walking into a club and I see them, I'll say 'Hey guys!' and they'll go, 'What? Oh my god, you noticed I was at the show!' That's something that always cracks me up. I'm watching them just as much as they're watching me."
>
> **CARRIE BROWNSTEIN, SLEATER-KINNEY**

towel, a pillow, and a sleeping bag. The usual rest: shampoo, toothbrush, your hair junk, etc. If you have an iPod (or whatever) bring it. Otherwise, you have to listen to whatever your bandmates are playing on the stereo or their long annoying cell phone conversations.

ON THE ROAD AGAIN

When you're on tour, you spend *a lot* of time on the road. Get ready
to plug in to your playlist. Here are some songs about touring, playing
shows, and being on the road:

★ **"Range Life"** Pavement

★ **"Tour Song"** Jawbreaker

★ **"Saturday Gigs"** Mott the Hoople

★ **"LT Tour Theme"** Le Tigre

★ **"The Road"** Jackson Browne

★ **"We're an American Band"**
Grand Funk Railroad

★ **"I've Been Everywhere"**
Johnny Cash

★ **"Banned in D.C."** Bad Brains

★ **"Sequestered in Memphis"**
The Hold Steady

★ **"Lodi"** Creedence Clearwater
Revival

★ **"Tour Spiel"** Minutemen

★ **"Turn The Page"** Bob Seger

★ **"On Tour With Zykos"**
Okkervil River

★ **"Award Tour"** A Tribe Called Quest

★ **"Homeward Bound"**
Simon and Garfunkel

★ **"All Ages Show"** Dag Nasty

★ **"Reunion Tour"** The Weakerthans

★ **"Lover I Don't Have to Love"**
Bright Eyes

★ **"On the Road"** Azita

★ **"Touring"** The Ramones

★ **"On the Road Again"**
Willie Nelson

★ **"But After the Gig"** Discharge

★ **"Thrasher"** Neil Young

★ **"Torn and Frayed"** Rolling Stones

★ **"Road Runner"** Jonathan Richman
& The Modern Lovers (okay, this one
is really just about driving with the
radio on)

Being in a confined space with people for hours and hours a day (even if you adore them and are BFFs till the end of time), you need some alone time. Headphones and your playlist are about as close as you'll get.

SOME OF THE THINGS I LOVED ABOUT TOURING

I'd traveled a lot before I ever went on tour, but touring is not like going on vacation. You are in one place for a day, maybe a day and a half. Sometimes the only part you get to explore is the area right around the club when you are searching for pizza before load-in. I was lucky that I was in a band with people who had toured a bunch so they knew where cool things were in every city we hit. They also liked to get to a city early so that we could explore, or if there was a cool museum or thing to see, we could check it out before we had to be at the show. If you can, make that part of your tour routine. Sometimes, there was nothing especially rad to do, but one of the best times I had on tour was just walking around Louisville looking at old buildings with a friend whose band we were touring with.

One morning I went out for a walk in Buffalo, New York, before anyone else had gotten up; there were some people doing a pirate radio broadcast on the sidewalk, and they interviewed me about how I was enjoying my time in Buffalo. It was 8 A.M. and one of them was playing a trombone. At that moment, I thought "If I was at home, I'd be asleep and missing this." Touring is *one big adventure*—it really is. You meet people and see all sorts of things that your friends who're spending their summer as counselors at soccer camp will never experience.

Being on tour with a band, especially if you are touring with

SAFETY FIRST

A couple on-the-road precautions:

1. If you are playing a big city, and there have been a rash of gear thefts after shows (you'll hear about it, if there has), drive a ways outside the city and get a hotel room, rather than risk getting your stuff stolen. This is a good idea in general.

2. Do not book a tour that takes you through the mountains in the middle of winter.

3. Learn to change a tire before you leave.

4. Get AAA. Aside from roadside assistance, you can get discounts on hotels and towing.

another band, is like being in a gang. You go everywhere in a pack—to the show, from the show, all of you in the same hotel room, to breakfast at Waffle House. After a few days of this, it starts to feel weird if you, for some strange reason, are by yourself. Eventually, by the end of the tour, it will get a little annoying not to have time alone, but it's nice to have a posse. The first long tour I did, our band toured with four other bands. In all, it was twenty-seven dudes—and me. It was great—having a giant pack of stinky brothers for a few weeks is a pretty amazing experience.

Touring made me think a lot about how much more freedom I have to pursue what I want than my grandmas ever did. My life at age twenty-six was already very different from theirs. I have been to almost every state in America, and had toured Japan, Canada, and Europe. Both of my grandmas had barely been anywhere outside of Indiana. When my mom was growing up in the '60s, most of the women you heard on the radio were singing songs that men had written for them—they weren't making their own music or performing songs that were about their own lives. It made me realize how different my life is from theirs—just because I'm in a band and making music that is mine.

WHY GO ON TOUR?

Aside from the adventure, touring is an investment in your fan base. If you are trying to have a career in music and turn it into more than a hobby, you must tour. To have a career, you need to have a fan base that supports you by buying your music and tickets to your shows. It might take nine long U.S. tours before you start to see a fan base or make any money, but fans are pretty loyal. If you put on a good show, and put out music that is worth spending money on, you can keep your fans for a long time.

APPENDIX A

ESSENTIALS OF ROCK: FOR YOUR LISTENING PLEASURE

You need to make sure that your musical education doesn't just revolve around learning chords or how to keep a steady beat. Here, to assist in your exploration and research, is a mini-guide of essential artists and recordings. Some are albums or artists that defined a genre—others are just the best record by a particularly influential act.

METAL

- **Slayer** *Reign in Blood*
- **Metallica** *Master of Puppets*
- **Sepultura** *Roots*
- **Motorhead** *Ace of Spades*
- **Black Sabbath** *Vol. 4 / Paranoid*
- **Runaways** *Queens of Noise*
- **Tool** *Undertow*
- **System of a Down** *System of a Down*
- **AC/DC** *Back in Black*
- **Deftones** *White Pony*

POP

- **Beach Boys** *Pet Sounds*
- **Madonna** *Madonna*
- **ABBA** *Gold*
- **Michael Jackson** *Thriller*
- **Boston** *Boston*
- **Yaz** *Upstairs at Eric's*

Prince

- **Prince** *Purple Rain*
- **The Zombies** *Odessey and Oracle*

6

RECORDS THAT CHANGED EVERYTHING

★ The Ramones *The Ramones*

★ Bob Dylan *Bringing It All Back Home*

★ The Beatles *Sgt. Pepper's Lonely Hearts Club Band*

★ Radiohead *OK Computer*

★ Public Enemy *It Takes a Nation ...*

★ Afrika Bambaataa and the Soulsonic Force *Planet Rock*

★ **Weezer** *Weezer (Blue Album)*

★ **Various Artists** *One Kiss Can Lead to Another: Girl Group Sounds Lost and Found*

PROGRESSIVE ROCK

★ **Magma** *Mekanik Destruktiw Kommandoh*

★ **Yes** *Fragile*

★ **Mars Volta** *De-Loused in the Comatorium*

★ **King Crimson** *In the Court of the Crimson King*

★ **Pink Floyd** *Dark Side of the Moon*

CLASSIC ROCK

★ **The Pretenders** *II*

★ **Rolling Stones** *Exile on Mainstreet*

★ **Neil Young** *Decade*

★ **The Kinks** *Village Green Preservation Society*

★ **Led Zeppelin** *IV*

★ **Fleetwood Mac** *Rumours*

★ **The Jimi Hendrix Experience** *Are You Experienced?, Axis: Bold As Love*

★ **Santana** *Abraxas*

★ **Grateful Dead** *American Beauty*

★ **Creedence Clearwater Revival** *Cosmo's Factory*

★ **Heart** *Dreamboat Annie*

★ **Buffalo Springfield** *Retrospective*

★ **Janis Joplin** *Pearl*

★ **The Beatles** *Revolver*

★ **The Who** *Who's Next?*

★ **David Bowie** *The Rise and Fall of Ziggy Stardust*

The Pretenders

GRUNGE

★ **Nirvana** *Bleach, Nevermind, In Utero*

★ **Pearl Jam** *Vs.*

★ **Hole** *Live Through This*

★ **Soundgarden** *Louder Than Love*

★ **Mudhoney** *Superfuzz Bigmuff*

FUNK

★ **James Brown** *Live at The Apollo, The Payback, 20 All Time Greatest Hits, Star Time*

★ **Labelle** *Nightbirds*

★ **Fela Kuti** *Zombie, Roforo Fight, Gentleman*

★ **Stevie Wonder** *Innervisions, Talking Book, Songs in the Key of Life*

★ **Funkadelic** *Maggot Brain, One Nation Under a Groove, Cosmic Slop*

★ **Parliament** *Chocolate City, Mothership Connection*

Betty Davis

★ **The Meters** *The Very Best of the Meters*

★ **Sly and The Family Stone** *There's a Riot Goin' On, Fresh!, Anthology*

★ **Betty Davis** *They Say I'm Different*

EARLY ROCK 'N' ROLL

★ **Little Richard** *The Very Best of Little Richard*

★ **Etta James** *At Last*

★ **Jerry Lee Lewis** *18 Original Sun Greatest Hits*

★ **Chuck Berry** *Gold*

★ **Gene Vincent** *The Screaming End: The Best of Gene Vincent*

★ **Ray Charles** *Modern Sounds in Country and Western Music*

- ★ **Ruth Brown** *The Best of Ruth Brown*
- ★ **Everly Brothers** *The Fabulous Style of the Everly Brothers*

BLUES

- ★ **Etta James** *At Last*
- ★ **Sister Rosetta Tharpe** *Complete Recorded Works Vol.1*
- ★ **Mississippi John Hurt** *Avalon Blues: The Complete 1928 Okeh Recordings*
- ★ **Skip James** *The Complete Early Recordings*
- ★ **Leadbelly** *The King of the 12-String Guitar*

Patti Smith

- ★ **Robert Johnson** *King of the Delta Blues*
- ★ **Memphis Minnie** *Hoodoo Lady 1933–1937*
- ★ **Bessie Smith** *The Complete Recordings*

PUNK

- ★ **The Ramones** *The Ramones*
- ★ **The Clash** *London Calling*
- ★ **Patti Smith** *Horses*
- ★ **X** *Los Angeles*
- ★ **The Avengers** *Died for Your Sins*
- ★ **The Stooges** *Raw Power*
- ★ **The Minutemen** *Double Nickels on the Dime*
- ★ **Fugazi** *13 Songs*
- ★ **Bikini Kill** *Reject All American*
- ★ **The Slits** *Cut*
- ★ **The Jam** *Compact Snap*
- ★ **Gang of Four** *Entertainment*

- ★ **X-Ray Spex** *Germ Free Adolescence*
- ★ **Bad Brains** *Bad Brains, Black Dots*
- ★ **Hüsker Dü** *Zen Arcade*
- ★ **Dead Kennedys** *Fresh Fruit for Rotting Vegetables*

GOTH

- ★ **Siouxsie & The Banshees** *The Scream*
- ★ **The Cure** *Staring at the Sea: The Singles*
- ★ **Joy Division** *Unknown Pleasures*
- ★ **Bauhaus** *Mask*
- ★ **Public Image Limited** *Flowers of Romance*

EXPERIMENTAL

- ★ **CAN** *Ege Bamyasi*
- ★ **Brian Eno** *Taking Tiger Mountain, Music for Airports*
- ★ **Diamanda Galas** *Plague Mass*
- ★ **Frank Zappa** *Hot Rats*

- ★ **Yoko Ono** *Yoko Ono/ Plastic Ono Band*
- ★ **Radiohead** *Ok Computer*
- ★ **Arthur Russell** *Calling Out of Context*

COUNTRY

- ★ **Hank Williams** *40 Greatest Hits*
- ★ **Johnny Cash** *At Folsom Prison*
- ★ **Patsy Cline** *The Patsy Cline Story*
- ★ **Loretta Lynn** *Greatest Hits*
- ★ **Dolly Parton** *Jolene, Coat of Many Colors*
- ★ **Merle Haggard** *The Best of The Best of Merle Haggard*
- ★ **The Carter Family** *1927–1934 (box set)*
- ★ **Linda Ronstadt** *Heart Like a Wheel*
- ★ **The Byrds** *Sweetheart of the Rodeo*

Joni Mitchell

FOLK

- ★ **Bob Dylan** *Bringing It All Back Home, Blonde on Blonde*
- ★ **Various Artists** *Anthology of American Folk Music Vols. 1–3*
- ★ **Joni Mitchell** *Blue*
- ★ **Woody Guthrie** *Dust Bowl Ballads*
- ★ **Odetta** *Best of the Vanguard Years*
- ★ **Nick Drake** *Five Leaves Left, Bryter Layter, Pink Moon*

SINGER-SONGWRITER

- ★ **Van Morrison** *Astral Weeks*

- ★ **Bob Dylan** *Highway 61 Revisited*
- ★ **PJ Harvey** *Rid of Me*
- ★ **Joni Mitchell** *Blue, Hissing of Summer Lawns*
- ★ **Carole King** *Tapestry*
- ★ **Joanna Newsom** *Ys*
- ★ **Tom Waits** *Rain Dogs*
- ★ **Neil Young** *On the Beach*
- ★ **Bruce Springsteen** *Nebraska*

JAZZ

- ★ **Miles Davis** *Kind of Blue, Bitches Brew, Sketches of Spain*
- ★ **John Coltrane** *A Love Supreme, Giant Steps, Ascension*
- ★ **Ornette Coleman** *The Shape of Jazz to Come, Free Jazz*
- ★ **Albert Ayler** *Spiritual Unity*
- ★ **Charles Mingus** *The Black Saint and the Sinner Lady*

⋆ **Sonny Rollins** *Saxophone Colossus*

⋆ **Sun Ra** *Atlantis*

⋆ **Patty Waters** *Sings*

⋆ **Billie Holiday** *Greatest Hits*

⋆ **Herbie Hancock** *Head Hunters*

⋆ **Nina Simone** *The Best of Nina Simone*

SOUL/R&B

⋆ **Aretha Franklin** *I Never Loved a Man the Way I Love You*

⋆ **Marvin Gaye** *What's Going On*

⋆ **Al Green** *I'm Still in Love with You*

⋆ **Stevie Wonder** *Songs in the Key of Life*

⋆ **Otis Redding** *Otis Blue*

⋆ **Donny Hathaway** *Extension of a Man*

⋆ **Roberta Flack & Donny Hathaway** *Roberta Flack & Donny Hathaway*

⋆ **The Staple Singers** *The Best of The Staple Singers*

⋆ **Dusty Springfield** *Dusty in Memphis*

⋆ **Sam Cooke** *Portrait of a Legend 1951–1964*

⋆ **Ray Charles** *The Birth of Soul: The Complete Atlantic R&B*

GLAM

⋆ **Lou Reed** *Transformer*

⋆ **Queen** *Sheer Heart Attack*

⋆ **T. Rex** *Electric Warrior*

⋆ **David Bowie** *Diamond Dogs*

⋆ **Brian Eno** *Here Come the Warm Jets*

⋆ **New York Dolls** *New York Dolls*

⋆ **Roxy Music** *Country Life*

POP PUNK

⋆ **Green Day** *Dookie*

⋆ **Paramore** *Riot!*

⋆ **Brand New** *Your Favorite Weapon*

⋆ **Descendents** *Milo Goes to College*

⋆ **Rancid** *Out Come the Wolves*

⋆ **Jawbreaker** *24 Hour Revenge Therapy*

EMO

⋆ **Sunny Day Real Estate** *Diary*

⋆ **Rites of Spring** *End on End*

⋆ **Fall Out Boy** *Take This to Your Grave*

⋆ **Cap'n Jazz** *Analphabetapolothology*

⋆ **Jawbreaker** *Dear You*

Dusty Springfield

MOVIES AND FILMS

The number of documentaries and films about music, genres, and bands seems infinite. Here's a list of some of the classics and must-sees to help you along, inspire you, and give you a sense of your place in rock history. Nearly all of these films are available through Netflix. *Note:* Some of these flicks deal with some kind of intense, adult themes, so check with your parents before watching them.

MOVIES

★ *Almost Famous* (2000, R): Teenage rock journalist goes on tour and learns life lessons.

★ *Blackboard Jungle* (1955, Not Rated): Movie's soundtrack helped popularize rock 'n' roll.

★ *Bound for Glory* (1976, PG): Woody Guthrie got his start as America's most celebrated folk singer in this biopic.

★ *Camp Rock* (2008, Not Rated) Demi Lovato and the Jonas Brothers star in this Disney story set at a rock 'n' roll summer camp.

★ *Coal Miner's Daughter* (1980, PG): Loretta Lynn biopic chronicles her rise from teen mom to one of the greatest country singers of all time.

★ *Desperate Teenage Lovedolls* (1984, Not Rated): Teenage girls form band and seek fame, but find trouble. Tons of cameos.

★ *Empire Records* (1995, PG-13): Day in the life of record store and its staff.

★ *A Hard Day's Night* (1964, G): The first Beatles movie, a classic day-in-the-life comedy.

★ *Head* (1968, G): Psychedelic art film starring The Monkees at their super weirdest.

★ *The Harder They Come* (1972, Not Rated): Jimmy Cliff stars as a struggling reggae singer in trouble in this classic film.

★ *High Fidelity* (2000, R): Record store clerk loses and finds love.

★ *High School Record* (2008, Not Rated): A faux-documentary about awkward high school outcasts, starring the front women of Mika Miko.

★ *Jubilee* (1978, Not Rated): Slightly experimental film that takes place in the early days of British punk and involves time traveling; features performances from The Slits, Siouxsie & The Banshees.

* *Ladies and Gentlemen, the Fabulous Stains* (1982, R): The quintessential girls-start-a-band-and-change-the-world movie.

* *Mystery Train* (1989, R): Elvis fans make pilgrimage to Memphis, hilarity ensues. Cameos from Screamin' Jay Hawkins and Joe Strummer.

* *Purple Rain* (1984, R): Classic film based on Prince's life and struggle to the top, starring Prince.

* *Quadrophenia* (1979, R): Mods battle Rockers in this rock opera based on The Who's album.

* *Rock 'n' Roll High School* (1979, PG): Spunky girl battles her principal with the help of The Ramones in this comedy.

* *The Rocky Horror Picture Show* (1975, R): Over-the-top rock 'n' roll musical, a cult classic.

* *The Rose* (1979, R): Bette Midler plays a mercurial rock singer in the mold of Janis Joplin.

* *The Sound of Music* (1965, G): Fractured family brought together by song escapes the Nazis.

* *Sweet Dreams* (1985, PG-13): The dramatic life story of Patsy Cline.

* *This Is Spinal Tap* (1984, R): Mockumentary about a fictional heavy metal band.

* *Times Square* (1980, R): Two girls form a band and try to change the world.

* *Tommy* (1975, PG): The Who's classic rock opera, featuring Tina Turner. One of the greatest music movies of all time.

* *What's Love Got To Do With It* (1993, R): Tina Turner's harrowing life story.

* *Wild Style* (1983, R): This low-budget classic captures the birth of hip-hop.

* *Xanadu* (1980, PG): A singing, dancing, roller-skating musical glitter fantasy starring Olivia Newton-John.

DOCUMENTARY/CONCERT FILMS

* *Afro-Punk* (2006, Not Rated): An overview of black punk.

* *All You Need Is Love: The Story of Popular Music* (1976, Not Rated): In-depth fourteen-hour history of pop music in all its forms, from its blues roots to glam.

* *Athens, GA—Inside/Out* (1987, Not Rated): A charming look at the small

but fruitful Athens scene, featuring REM and the B-52's.

★ *The !!!! Beat* (1966, Not Rated): Short-lived but amazing Houston TV show features live performances from dozens of R&B greats, including Etta James and Carla Thomas.

★ *Bob Dylan: Don't Look Back* (1965, Not Rated): Informal behind-the-scenes look at Dylan in all his weirdness, at the start of his fame.

★ *The Clash: Westway to the World* (2000, Not Rated): Quintessential Clash documentary with interviews and tons of great live footage.

★ *The Complete Monterey Pop Festival* (1968, Not Rated): Behind the scenes and live footage of this major 1967 festival, includes must-see Janis Joplin and Jimi Hendrix performances.

★ *The Devil and Daniel Johnston* (2005, PG-13): The incredible and sad story of Daniel Johnston's talent and mental illness.

★ *Festival Express* (2004, R): Lost concert film from 1970 featuring Grateful Dead and Janis Joplin footage.

★ *The Filth and The Fury: A Sex Pistols Film* (2000, R): The real story of the band's brief, explosive career also serves as a cautionary tale.

★ *Girls Rock!* (2007, PG): Inspirational behind-the-scenes journey to Portland's Rock Camp for Girls.

★ *Heavy Metal Parking Lot* (1986, Not Rated): Cult classic documentary/accidental comedy about metal fans in the parking lot of a Judas Priest show.

★ *Instrument: Ten Years with the Band Fugazi* (2001, Not Rated): A loose documentary weaves together awesome live footage with life on the road.

★ *Jazz on a Summer's Day* (1960, Not Rated): Concert film of the Newport Jazz Festival with all the big names in jazz, plus awesome performances by Big Maybelle and Mahalia Jackson.

★ *The Last Waltz* (1978, PG): The Band does a long farewell concert, with show-stealing performances from friends including The Staple Singers and Joni Mitchell.

★ *Led Zeppelin* (2003, Not Rated): A compilation of concert and TV footage from 1970–79, plus some of the best stuff from their 1973 concert film, *The Song Remains the Same*.

Les Paul: Chasing Sound (2007, Not Rated): A look at how Les Paul helped popularize electric guitars and modern recording techniques; a crucial part of rock history.

Metallica: Some Kind of Monster (2004, R): Intense behind-the-scenes Metallica documentary shows the dark side of fame.

The Night James Brown Saved Boston (2008, Not Rated): A documentary about how the broadcast of a James Brown concert prevented riots in Boston after the assassination of Martin Luther King in 1968, and music's role in the struggle for civil rights.

1991: The Year Punk Broke (1991, Not Rated): Sonic Youth tour with Nirvana, Babes in Toyland, and Hole.

Parliament Funkadelic: The Mothership Connection: 1976 Live (1976, Not Rated): Must-see concert footage of P-Funk in all their sweaty, costumed, spaceship-riding glory.

Patti Smith: Dream of Life (2008, Not Rated): An up-close-and-personal look at Patti Smith's expansive career, with concert footage.

PJ Harvey on Tour: Please Leave Quietly (2005, Not Rated): A raw, collage-like film capturing her 2004 tour.

Radiohead: Meeting People Is Easy (1999, Not Rated): Radiohead plays show, deals with the burden of fame.

The Rolling Stones: Gimme Shelter (1970, R): The highs and lows of the Stones' 1969 tour. A classic.

Wattstax (1973, R): Classic R&B/soul concert film that documents the era as well as the music.

We Jam Econo: The Story of the Minutemen (2005, Not Rated): More than a documentary of the influential band, it's a movie about friendship and the D.I.Y. spirit.

Wild Combination: A Portrait of Arthur Russell (2008, Not Rated): An overview of the inspiring life and premature death of Arthur Russell, a singer, songwriter, cellist, avant-garde composer, and disco producer.

Woodstock: 3 Days of Peace & Music (1970, R): The chaotic concert that defined the '60s.

X: The Unheard Music (1985, R): Chronicles the leading light of LA's punk scene, X.

APPENDIX B

IN THE GARAGE: GETTING STARTED IN GARAGEBAND

Here's a primer on how to get rolling with GarageBand, and ways to produce and mix your songs.

TEMPO

Open up GarageBand on your computer. Before you start writing and recording your song, the first thing to figure out is the *tempo*, or the pace, of the song. The reason you want to do that is so that each track you record can be synced together later without it sounding out of time (which would be like one person being out of step in a marching band). If you're only using virtual instruments, you can change the tempo later on. With real instruments, however, you are locked in at the tempo you record in. This is why it's good to decide your tempo before getting too far along in creating your song.

BPM When you hit record in the program, you'll hear this little beat called the click track. It's to help you play in time and it's set to record at default tempo of 120 beats per minute (bpm).

If you don't know what tempo you want, hit the record button—and on the counter window, click on the arrow above the note icon until you see the tempo setting. Click where it says 120, and stop and adjust it. A very slow song would be 60 bpm, 85 is mid-tempo, 110–140 is rock song range, above 140 is considered fast. Above 140 is the bpm for a lot of techno music and hard-core bands.

Meter The second step is to figure out

if the song is going to be in 3/4 or 4/4 time. Three-four (3/4) time means that there are three beats in a measure; 4/4 time means there are four. There are other times to choose from, but they are all essentially variations on 3/4 (commonly called "waltz time"—see also "Happy Birthday" and the beginning of The Beatles' "Lucy in the Sky with Diamonds") and 4/4 (ex. 6/4, 2/4, 6/8, 12/8). Almost all pop, rock, and hip-hop is in 4/4, meaning there are four beats, each equivalent to one quarter note, in a measure.

FIRST THINGS FIRST

The rhythm is the basis for most rock songs, so the first thing you record are the rhythm tracks. That means drums come first, and here's how that needs to go down:

Using Live Drums

For recording live drums, set up your mic and plug it into your mixer. You'll probably want to play drums along to the click track that GarageBand gives you. If you are going to record tracks of virtual instruments later, it's best if the rhythm bed was done to a click track, because then everything will be in sync. Live drums can't be "quantized" (a.k.a. fixed by the computer). To play along with the click track, plug your headphones into your computer, hit "record," and turn up the volume until you can hear its tick-tock over your playing.

Click Tracks and Human Drummers

Some drummers resist playing to click tracks because it makes their playing *too* exact; for some, it takes the swing out of their playing. You might be one of those drummers. Or maybe you have perfect, natural time and the click is unnecessary. If you are only recording live instruments, and not using any of the virtual instruments, you may be perfectly fine playing by feel. Most people slow down and speed up and have little rhythmic hiccups when they play. It's good to learn to play to a click track. It can be a little humiliating at first because with every click you are suddenly aware of how off your own timing is. Once you get the hang of playing, it's really helpful because the firmer your timing and tempo is, the better everything sounds.

Using the Drums That Live Inside the Computer

Once you're in the track menu, go to "new track." When asked whether you want to use software (virtual) or real instruments; click on "software."

1 If the options window for instruments doesn't show, hit the "i" icon at the bottom right, (track info) and choose your instrument.

2 Go to drum kits, and select the one you like. Keep in mind you can change it later.

3 Click the red circle at the top left, and it will arm the track with the instrument you've picked out.

4 Go to the window menu and select Musical Typing from the menu. This will bring up the musical typing window. This lets your computer's keyboard mimic a musical keyboard. You can use the Z and X keys to change octaves.

5 Experiment with the sounds on the kit, and practice the beat that you want to play.

When you are ready, press the record button at the bottom of the window (the transport). Once you hear the click track, "play" (type) your beat. You don't have to record the beat for the whole song, you can just record two good measures and then "loop" it (so it repeats). If you don't like what you've come up with or you mess up, just stop (space bar) and undo (⌘ + Z). After you have recorded a measure or two that came out how you wanted, double click on the region of notes you just recorded, and that will bring up the track editor at the bottom. You want to "quantize" (accurately lock into the tempo what you just played). If you don't, and your rhythm is off, it's going to throw everything in the song off, and will make your loops weird. Not good weird—annoying weird.

To quantize:

1 Go to the edit menu and select all; this selects the notes.

2 On the track editor at the bottom, under the "Advanced" header (you might need to click the arrow at the right of the "Track" header if "Advanced" is hidden) it says "Auto Align to:" and has a drop-down menu to select the level of quantization.

3 Choose 16th note. The vast majority of the time, quantizing to the 16th will clean things up perfectly. What this does is snap the notes into the nearest 16th note, which just cleans up any slowing/speeding.

4 Listen to it again—it should sound great—now it's sharp and so very quantized.

Making Your (Rhythm) Bed

Go back to the track window, and put your cursor at the top right corner of the region of notes. The cursor will change into a curved arrow symbol. Click and drag that for as long as you want to have that part repeat. With this action, you have just made a rhythm bed.

THE REST

Unless your band is a drums-only band (great idea, for sure), you want to start adding other tracks of instruments. Go to the track menu and select new track, and repeat what you just did—choose real or virtual instruments, record, and then quantize to the 16th.

When you are recording a new track with real instruments, make sure your speakers (if you are using them) are off and your headphones are connected to your computer. You want to hear the playback in the headphones only. In the track info window, on the bottom right, switch monitor to "on." Then you can hear yourself while you are recording (if you want). Before you start, try to play as loudly as you will play during the recording, and make sure the meter stays out of the red (or you'll get a distorted signal).

Troubleshooting It's common to have problems when you try to record into the computer. The key to figuring out what's wrong is to eliminate what isn't wrong first. If you can see the meters moving but you can't hear your instrument in your headphones, you know that the problem isn't between the microphone and your computer. In that case, you would check that the volume is turned up and that your headphones are plugged in correctly. If you can't see the meters moving when you play your instrument, make sure that the "record enable" dot is red, and that your microphone is plugged in correctly.

GARAGEBAND MIX-DOWN

Mixing is where you take all the tracks you have recorded (drums, bass, vocals, etc.) and funnel them down to two channels (left and right). You add effects (like compression or reverb) to add details and make things sound better or different; you are tailoring the sound. If you don't mix a song and just leave it the way you recorded it, it'll sound a little weird because the vocals and drums are louder than all the other instruments. When you record, everything is going in at different levels, and in the final mix you want them in their right places.

Mixing is another part of your creative process. The main thing is: Trust your ears—they're smart. When sound moves in certain ways around you, your mind automatically envisions what sort of room-space it's in. This is the really cool thing about mixing; you are creating this mini-world for your song to exist in. You are conjuring up a layer around your song, and each person that hears it is going to imagine it a little differently.

THIS STRANGE EFFECT: THE MAIN EFFECTS TO USE WHEN YOU ARE MIXING

Compression—It adjusts the loud and quiet parts so they're not so extreme; it's mainly used to tame loud parts so they don't roar up out of nowhere. Compression should always be used on vocals and sometimes on drums; it's also important to use on the bass, because there are spots on the bass fret board that are louder than the rest.

Reverb—This effect simulates a room environment. It can make things sound farther away. Imagine what it sounds like when you clap you hands in your room, and how it sounds when you clap in an empty hallway, and how it sounds when you do it in a gymnasium. Reverb can make things sound like they were recorded in a different space. It can make the vocal track you did in the bathroom sound like you recorded it in a cathedral.

Echo/Delay—The echo feature creates an echo (and I know you know what that is). Delay is like echo but more drawn-out.

Tremolo—This effect is a fast, repeating volume swell.

Overdrive/Distortion—This effect makes things sound dirtier, more intense, and thrashier. Originally, distortion was used—or made—by blues musicians, when they first switched to electric guitars. They would slash the front of their amp speaker and it would sound scuzzy and torn when they played through it. A lot of things sound good with distortion on them; personally, I believe distortion is the salt of sound effects—it makes everything better.

Thinking in 3-D

When you're mixing, it helps to imagine the song as being three-dimensional—like it's a big box *around* you. The different dimensions of this box are a) left and right, b) front and back, and c) top and bottom. Creative mixing uses all three.

You adjust left and right with the pan knob. You can make a sound, track, or instrument go all the way to the left or right of a mix, or have it in the middle (equally in both sides). With headphones, you can hear how things are panned by taking one headphone off your ear; the guitar might be on the left and the vocals on the right, and the drums might be equally in both.

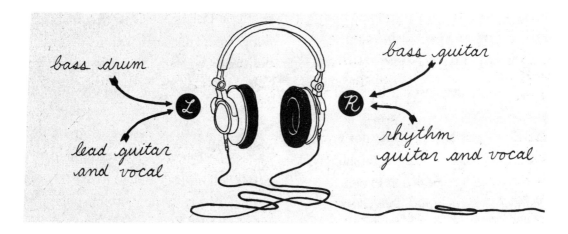

bass drum

bass guitar

lead guitar
and vocal

rhythm
guitar and vocal

You get front and back dimensions by using volume, reverb, and other effects that affect how close something sounds. You can make quiet sounds louder, so it seems like they are happening very close to you. You can put reverb on drums and make them sound big or like they are farther away. Let's say you've created a song with whisper-quiet vocals and a distorted guitar that gets louder and louder in the mix as the song goes on. In the mix, you turn the vocals up and the guitar down, so it starts out soft and grows into a wall of sound. If you close your eyes and listen to that on your headphones, it's going to sound like the person singing is RIGHT THERE telling a secret, and the guitar will sound like it's approaching and then exploding.

For top and bottom, you adjust the EQ (equalizer). A try-this-at-home example of how to understand EQ: When someone is sitting facing you and talking, you are just hearing the one sound wave—her voice going toward you. Now, if she gets up and backs away, across the room, and talks to you as she moves, her voice sounds different—you are not only hearing the sound of her voice but also her voice bouncing off the walls. When you are sitting close, you hear the dynamic range of her voice, which means it'll sound fuller and lower. When she moves away, her voice will sound more mid-range; you won't hear as much low sound in it.

There is a technique to try out when you are mixing that is simple and can make things sound pretty cool, swiped from The Ramones. On their first album, all the instruments are panned either all the way left or right or in the center. If you listen on just one speaker or one headphone, you'll hear only one of two different instruments or vocal tracks that occupy the same frequency range. The Beatles also did this. See the diagram, top left, for reference.

In each ear, there will be a low frequency instrument and a high one, but it's not the same on both sides. This is good/easy separation, but it also keeps the frequencies from interfering with each other and sounding muddy; which brings us to our next hot topic: the mud.

Mud, Honey

The "mud" frequency is your enemy, your song's enemy, and your mix's enemy. It won't ruin what you are making, but things will sound pretty bad to whoever's listening. The mud frequency exists between 300 and 400 Hz (see box, next page). When you are recording with a couple of instruments, you are going to build up a lot of sound at that 300 to 400 frequency. As that builds up, your mix will start to sound muddy, wompy, and possibly

blobbish. To avoid dragging your song into downtown mud town, turn down the frequency range on some or most of the instruments when you are EQing the tracks, and you'll avoid a muddy mix.

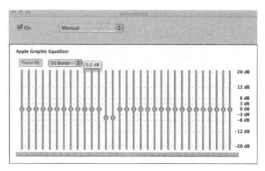

Distortion

When you are mixing down, always make sure to keep an eye on your *meter*. In GarageBand, the meter is at the bottom, next to the counter. On other programs or on a regular mixing console, you always want to make sure the needle on the levels doesn't peak into the red. If it's in the red, it's distorted.

Audio distortion means what went in is not being spit back out accurately. In the case of the song you're mixing, it's coming out too "hot" (loud). Distortion as an effect is infinitely awesome, but when distortion is unintended, it means bad news for your mix.

LOVE HERTZ!

Hertz (Hz), pronounced "hurts" is the unit of measure of audio frequency. The low numbers of Hz are the low, bass frequencies and a high-pitched frequency would be something like 12,000 Hz (or 12 kHz; you add the k once you are in the thousands). When we are born, the frequency range of our hearing is really broad. A newborn can hear from 20 Hz to 20,000 kHz. Hearing gets worse as we get older, so for someone who is thirty-five, they might be able to only hear up to 18,000 kHz. Now, here is the best part, lucky for you and me: *Women hear better than men.* We hear higher frequencies for more of our lives, and we sustain less hearing loss than men. All the better for your mix, and/or your future career as a producer. If a sound guy or dude engineer ever gives you any dispute, feel free to remind him that you have a more dynamic range of hearing. Throw those extra Hz in his face.

Once you've got your mix levels worked out, it's time to output this song from GarageBand and into the free world. You are going to put it on a CD, turn it into an MP3, or export it into your iTunes. Go to the share menu. It'll ask you if you want to export a CD quality version or a lower quality version. Which way you save it is up to you, and it depends on what you want to do with it. Saving it to CD quality is high quality; it's going to sound the best. You can reduce that down to MP3 quality (okay quality) later if you need to. If you save it first as an MP3, you can't improve the quality back up to CD quality.

WEIRDO RIPPERS: MP3 SOUND QUALITY

No matter what level you choose to rip your song at, if you are choosing MP3 quality, you are choosing a lesser quality. The bit rates (320, 256, 192) are just grades of quality—the higher the number being the better quality. You will be able to hear the difference between 320 and 192. An MP3 is like a bad Xerox; it's the song at a lower resolution, and its audio is going to be kind of blurry.

MY ROCK PROFILE

Fill in the blanks below to learn more about yourself as a musician. Set goals, reach far, rock hard, and refer back to it from time to time to see how your answers and perspectives have changed. (Hey, when you become famous, your biographer might want to see what you were up to when you first started.)

"INSPIRATION INFORMATION" —Shuggie Otis

★ My name is _____.

★ The name of my band is _____.

★ I play _____.

★ I have been playing for _____ days/weeks/months/years (circle one).

★ My band sounds like _____.

★ Our main influences are _____.

★ The first song I ever wrote is called _____
and it is about _____
_____.

★ It was an easy/hard (circle one) song for me to write because _____
_____
_____.

★ My favorite songs are:

_____ by _____

_____ by _____

_____ by _____

_____ by _____

_____ by _____

★ The one song can't stop listening to is _____

by _____. I can't stop listening to it because _____

_____

_____.

★ My rock idols are: _____

_____

_____.

★ I admire him/her/them because: _____

_____

_____.

★ My new favorite band is: _____.

★ My old favorite band is: _____.

"I'VE GOT DREAMS TO REMEMBER" —Otis Redding

★ My favorite thing that I have learned so far is _____

_____.

★ My biggest challenge as a musician is _____

_____.

★ My dream for my band is _____.

★ My artistic goals are:

1. _____.
2. _____.
3. _____.

★ The top three other instruments I want to learn how to play are:

1. _____.
2. _____.
3. _____.

"WISH FULFILLMENT" —Sonic Youth

★ If I could be in a band with any musician(s) in the world, here is my lineup: _____
_____.

★ If I had to come up with an album today it would be called _____
_____ and it would sound like _____
_____.

★ If I could play any venue in the world from a giant stadium to a grassy field to a tiny
music club, it would be _____.

"REASON TO BELIEVE" —Tim Hardin

★ My favorite thing about being in a band is _____
_____.

★ The things that inspire me to make music are _____
_____

★ The reason making music is so important to me is _____
_____

ABOUT THE AUTHOR

Jessica Hopper is a music and culture critic whose work regularly appears in the *Chicago Reader, LA Weekly, SPIN, ANP Quarterly,* and the *Chicago Tribune,* and has also been included in *DaCapo Best Music Writing 2004, 2005,* and *2007.* She is also the music consultant for the public radio show *This American Life.* Her widely anthologized essay, "Emo: Where the Girls Aren't" was described as "influential" by *The New York Times.*

Holding fast to the music-is-my-life credo, Hopper has also done time as a tour manager, band publicist, DJ, touring bassist, and fanzine publisher. She lives in Chicago.

CREDITS

Special thanks to Forever 21 for main cover wardrobe.

COVER

FRONT: Main cover photography by Gabrielle Revere; Background by vnlit/Shutterstock; Upper left photo spot by Somos/Veer; Left center spot by Bogden Ionescu/Shutterstock.

BACK: Lower right photo by Somos/Veer/Getty Images; upper left photo by Gabrielle Revere.

PHOTO CREDITS

INTERIOR: age fotostock: Juice Images p. 44; Michael DeWitt: p. 133; Getty Images: Mick Gold/Redferns p. iii, p. 23, 187, Bob Berg p. 27, Steve Eichner p. 26, Evening Standard/Stringer p. 211, Girl Ray p. 90; Scott Gries p. 99, Simon Horswell p. 181, Hulton Archive p. 163, Jeffrey Mayer/WireImage p. 111, Ethan Miller p. 128, Tim Mosenfelder p. 34, Paul Natkin p. 206, Michael Ochs Archives/Stringer p. viii (bottom), 49, 50, 53, 81, 108, 131,152, 208, 209, Jack Robinson p. 210, George Rose p. 142, 207, John Shearer/WireImage p. viii (top), 29, 85, 182, Ray Tamarra p. 24, Chris Walter/WireImage p. 38, 135, Karl Walter p. 82, Theo Wargo/WireImage p. 89, Kevin Winter p. ix; John Hopper: p. 193; Dan Monick: p. 148; Photofest: Paramount Pictures p. 101; *Punk Is Dead Punk Is Everything* (show flyers reprinted with permission of the author, Bryan Turcotte, and Gingko Press) p. 161; Retna Ltd: Larry Busacca p. 58, Barry Schultz/Sunshine p. 184; Gabrielle Revere: p. 46, 86, 205; Mike Rock: p. 104.

TIMELINE: Getty Images: Waring Abbott/Michael Ochs Archives 1976 (The Runaways), Archive Photos 1982 (Joan Jett), Tom Copi/Michael Ochs Archives 1952, Frank Driggs Collection 1923, Jill Gibson/Michael Ochs Archive 1967, Tim Graham 1983 (Karen Carpenter), Lisa Haun/Michael Ochs Archives 1980, Jason Kemplin/FilmMagic 2007, Chuck Krall/Michael Ochs Archives 1975, Jeff Kravitz/FilmMagic 1993 (The Breeders), Lichfield 1978, Terry Lott/Sony Music Archive 1983 (Cyndi Lauper), Tom Maday/Time Life Pictures 1993 (Liz Phair), Kevin Mazur/WireImage 1991, Frank Micelotta/ImageDirect 1995, Michael Ochs Archives 1939, 1963, 1964, 1966, 1974 (Etta James), 1974 (LaBelle), 1981, Randall Michelson/WireImage 2008 (Kimya Dawson), Tim Mosenfelder 2008 (Camp Rock), PhotoNews International Inc./FilmMagic 2008 (Pink), Robin Platzer/Time Life Pictures 1980 (Blondie), George Rose 1976 (Dreamboat Annie), Michael Schwartz/WireImage 1969, Jim Steinfeldt/Michael Ochs Archives 1982 (Bow Wow Wow), Marty Temme/WireImage 1971 (Carole King), Chris Walter/WireImage 1971 (Joni Mitchell), 1980 (The Pretenders); PR Photos: Daniel Locke 2001, 2003.

AUTHOR PHOTO: Dan Monick

LYRIC CREDITS

"Benton Harbor Blues": Written by Matthew Friedberger and Eleanor Friedberger. Published by Friedberger and Friedberger (ASCAP), administered by Domino Publishing Company USA (ASCAP). Printed by permission, courtesy of Matthew and Eleanor Friedberger. "Free Ride": Words and music by Dan Hartman. Copyright © 1972, 1974 (Renewed 2000, 2002) EMI Blackwood Music, Inc. All rights reserved. International copyright secured. Used by permission. "Be My Baby": Words and music by Phil Spector, Ellie Greenwich and Jeff Barry. Copyright © 1963 (Renewed) Trio Music Company, Universal-Songs of Polygram International, Inc. and Mother Bertha Music, Inc. All rights for Mother Bertha Music, Inc. controlled and administered by EMI April Music, Inc. All rights reserved. "I Apologize": Written by Bob Mould. Copyright © 1985 Granary Music (BMI)/Administered by Bug Music. All rights reserved. Used by permission. "London Calling": Words and music by Joe Strummer, Mick Jones, Paul Simonon and Topper Headon. Copyright © 1979 Nineden Ltd. All Rights in he U.S. and Canada controlled and administered by Universal-Polygram International Publishing, Inc. All rights reserved. Used by permission.